The Transition Tightrope

Supporting students in transition to secondary school

Angie Wilcock

 Routledge
Taylor & Francis Group

LONDON AND NEW YORK

First published 2013
by Routledge
2 Park Square, Milton Park, Abingdon, Oxon OX14 4RN

Simultaneously published in the USA and Canada
by Routledge
711 Third Avenue, New York, NY 10017

Routledge is an imprint of the Taylor & Francis Group, an informa business

British Library Cataloguing in Publication Data
A catalogue record for this book is available from the British Library

Library of Congress Cataloging in Publication Data
Wilcock, Angie.
The transition tightrope: supporting students in transition to secondary schools / Angie Wilcock.
p. cm.
Includes bibliographical references and index.
1. Articulation (Education)—Great Britain. 2. Education, Primary—Great Britain. 3. Education, Secondary—Great Britain. 4. Student adjustment—Great Britain. I. Title.
LB1626.W55 2012
371.2'83—dc23
2012017800

ISBN: 978-0-415-63436-6 (hbk)
ISBN: 978-0-415-63437-3 (pbk)
ISBN: 978-0-203-08408-3 (ebk)

Typeset in Sabon 10/13pt
by Book Now Ltd, London

MIX
Paper from responsible sources
FSC
www.fsc.org   FSC® C004839

Printed and bound by CPI Group (UK) Ltd, Croydon, CR0 4YY

The Transition Tightrope

The transition phase from primary to secondary school is a time of massive personal, physical, psychological and social change. Not only is it a difficult time for the young adolescent, but it is also a challenging time for parents, teachers and anyone working with young people experiencing such substantial changes in their lives. In this highly accessible book, Angie Wilcock offers clear, practical and realistic tips and strategies to support teachers' and parents' understanding of this difficult transition stage.

If you are concerned that your child or pupil may have difficulty coping with the many changes and challenges associated with this phase, this book will give you insight into issues such as:

- understanding the developing teen and effective ways to handle them;
- keeping up with multiple assignments;
- creating a system of organisation and an effective work space at home;
- maintaining a healthy balance between work, play…and sleep!;
- developing a positive attitude to school and study;
- setting realistic goals;
- making new friends;
- establishing life skills which are transferable to school.

Based on real-life teaching and parenting experience and full of practical, helpful case studies, this is just the resource you need to help you support and guide your developing teen.

Angie Wilcock is a teacher, parent and a respected authority on transition from primary to secondary education. She develops and presents information sessions and workshops to parents, students and teachers on a range of educational issues.

80003285111

Commendation – Dr Neil Hawkes

"I am delighted to commend this insightful book about transition to **every** parent and educator. I was privileged to hear Angie talk on this subject at a major conference in Hobart, Australia. Her grasp of the issues grabbed my attention and evidently helped to transform the thinking and understanding of her audience. Many young people are going to be indirectly helped because of this clearly written and engaging book. Brilliant!"

Dr Neil Hawkes DPhil (Oxford)
International Consultant for Education and Leadership and Visiting Fellow Bristol University, Graduate School of Education, UK.

To Dad. A hero, whose calm resolve to tackle insurmountable challenge and change head-on was an inspiration to all who knew and loved him.

Contents

Foreword   ix
Preface   xi
Acknowledgements   xiii
Building success in secondary school   xv

Introduction – what the research says about transition   1

1 The middle years – morphing from gorgeous to grumpy   3

2 Girls and boys – *vive la différence*!   11

3 The new social network – real friends, not online!   17

4 Parents keeping a connection with their school   23

5 Aligning the stars – finding that balance between
   work and play   33

6 Work environment – basic or brilliant?   45

7 "Where's my assignment?" – the need to be organised   53

8 Managing time – it can be done!   61

9 Attitude – "What attitude?"   73

10 Parents with style – which style suits you?   85

11 See it...hear it...do it – working smarter, not harder   93

12 The art of setting goals   101

Epilogue – the last word   107

Notes   109
Bibliography   113
Index   115

Foreword

It's a fact. The dynamics of secondary schooling are different. Kids are often keen to cut the apron strings and go it alone. Parents often bow out of the scene – because they're time poor, or feel that they've done their job, or realise they can't help much with academic studies anymore. Often enough, too, schools have narrow views about what parents should or should not do to support learning and schooling. Yet, as Angie says, well-informed and engaged parents can make a really critical difference as children transition to secondary school and move onwards.

A rich source of practical ideas, *The Transition Tightrope* provides a great road map for anyone who wants to better support young people to learn and succeed in school.

Caz Bosch
President, Australian Parents Council

Preface

The leap to secondary school

Life as a parent is all about changing and growing with your children. From the first moment we become parents to that moment when our son or daughter flies from the nest to the big world beyond, change is inevitable and sometimes overwhelming for parents.

Sometimes it seems that the goalposts keep changing; that the world we lived in as youngsters has transformed into something we don't even recognise, yet we have the responsibility of not only navigating our own way through it, but also guiding our children towards good choices and positive outcomes.

Every parent will experience major events with their children and one of them is the transition to secondary school. This transition is far more than simply relocating to a larger campus, having multiple teachers, experiencing new learning outcomes and subjects, finding new friends or catching a different bus to school. It is a time of significant change – not just academically, but also physically, emotionally, socially and cognitively.

I have been a classroom teacher for more than twenty years and am a mother of two sons. Despite my inside knowledge of education and my many years of teaching and dealing with children and families in the final phase of primary education, it is not until you experience it with your own child that you appreciate the change. The more informed we are about these changes, the more we can support and guide our children through them.

So many parents comment that both they and their children feel inadequately prepared for secondary school: "We weren't ready for this!" is a common cry. With an extensive curriculum to cover, teachers in general have little, if any, time to go beyond what is required and communication between secondary schools and primary schools is often not as strong as it could be.

Children and parents sometimes feel caught in the middle – the gap between primary and secondary school can look pretty scary when you're ready to leave the security of your primary school to enter the world of secondary school, with potentially 179 new Year 7 students to meet!

I have often asked educators and parents alike this question:

> How would you feel if, after seven years, you moved from a comfy, well-established workplace of 30 colleagues to an office of 180 – many of whom you have never met before – and are expected to slip quickly into a productive role?

It's this kind of perspective that pulls us up by the bootstraps and makes us realise that not only do our children need effective intervention from the education quarter, but parents need to be more informed as well.

Once we recognise that 'transition' is a phase, and not just a brief period of 'orientation' to new beginnings, we can begin to address the specific needs of students and their parents. I have worked personally with many students, some as advanced as Year 10, who simply have not transitioned as well as they might, and are still struggling with the demands of secondary school.

So, after several years of working with thousands of families across Australia and listening to their stories and their concerns, I decided it was about time parents discovered they were not alone; they were not over-reacting to these changes. There is a need for more information and the need is very real.

This is a book for all parents, regardless of personal memories of successes or failures at school; regardless of advantage or disadvantage; regardless of how much you think you know or don't know about how schools work these days.

Whether you are parents, teachers, counsellors or indeed anyone who lives or works with young people, I hope that the message here is both clear and powerful – you *do* matter and you *do* make a difference.

After all, who knows our children better than us?

Acknowledgements

This book started as a passing thought and became a dripping tap which could not be ignored. It has been written as a tribute to all those thousands of parents who not only offer their hearts and souls to their children, but also advice that often seems to fall on deaf ears!

I have shared personal stories, as well as objective research and advice, and I thank my boys, Adam and Ben, for their generosity in allowing their own stories to be told. I also thank those whose stories inspired me as examples of humour, dilemma, choices and just plain growing up.

I would like to acknowledge my patient, loving husband, Ross, who both accepts and encourages my strong will and relentless talking, and who has inspired me to pursue what was originally an interest that turned into a full-blown change of career.

My mum, at 83, has been a constant source of love, motivation and encouragement – which proves that, at any age, we still need and value our parents.

Finally, a huge thank you to the team at Routledge for their commitment and faith in publishing this book, as well as their tireless efforts in production and final publication.

Building success in secondary school

Being successful in secondary school is not all about high scores and academic achievement. There are many factors which contribute to a feeling of *success*, most of which have little, if anything, to do with test scores. If we teach, live or work with young people in transition to secondary school, consider this pyramid as a series of building blocks – stepping stones to becoming a more motivated and *successful teen*!

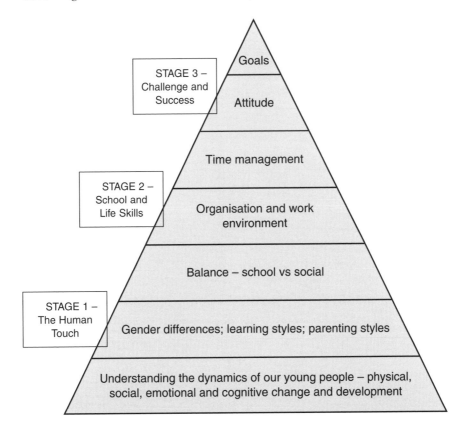

Introduction – what the research says about transition

Research suggests that achievement experienced by students in their final primary years can suddenly nosedive on entry into secondary school. There are a variety of reasons for this initial decline and ongoing struggle for some students, right up to Year 9, to make sense of their world at school. Hill and Russell[1] concluded that during this period there is student *decline* in:

- positive attitude towards school;
- satisfaction with school;
- perceived support from school;
- perceived levels of respect by teachers;
- interest and engagement in learning.

There is a wealth of research and studies out there, conducted over the past 30 years or so, which identify this period as quite unique, and yet quite challenging for students, parents and teachers alike. This leap from primary to secondary school coincides with massive personal, social and educational change. Motivation during this middle years phase (10–15 years) is associated with "a heightened awareness of emerging adulthood".[2]

Dr Andrew Martin, an Australian psychologist who specialises in student motivation, believes that if we have a good relationship with our children, then "up to half the work is done".[3] Student motivation and achievement is not only affected by parents' attitudes and expectations, but also by the relationship between parent and child.

If we are to promote a successful transition to secondary school and a continued positive journey throughout these years at school, we need to find every opportunity we can to build success into their lives and take every opportunity to challenge their negative thinking – and by so doing, increase their self-belief.[4]

So, what does this mean in terms of how parents can assist their child during this critical phase? The old saying "to be forewarned is to be forearmed" has never made more sense.

In terms of addressing student needs at the school level, we expect that both institutions and educators will identify the specific needs of students in this transition and middle years phase, and set about supporting change. Strategies which address changes to school culture, organisation, curriculum, learning, teaching and assessment practices can reverse the trend of disengagement.

For parents, increased knowledge, awareness and an understanding of their child's developmental changes can soothe the anxieties associated with the manifestation of these changes at home.

So, when your son or daughter says "I hate school!", *don't* say "I did too!" or "Too bad, you have six years to go!" – use some of your prior knowledge, experience and understanding to counter these claims with some positive parenting. As parents of high schoolers, particularly those of first-time high schoolers, now is the time to step *up*, not step back.

A 2008 UK study commissioned by the British Educational Communications and Technology Agency[5] on parent engagement concluded that parental interest in their child's education makes a powerful impact on children's learning and achievement. With an understanding of what makes our children 'tick', and the confidence to implement practical strategies at home, *we* are our child's best teacher.

Professor Mel Levine, author of *Ready or Not, Here Life Comes*, believes that successful transitions to secondary school rely very heavily on strong family ties and effective communication and that "kids thrive on the right mix of positive and negative reinforcement".[6] He also claims that "they need to feel they perform well for an appreciative, yet constructively critical audience. And there's no more influential and motivating audience than their parents".[7]

If we can continue to strengthen these relationships throughout secondary school and adolescence – and accept that we will lose battles along the way – the results can be amazing!

Chapter 1

The middle years – morphing from gorgeous to grumpy

"Who *are* you?"

The 'middle years' refer to students in Years 5–9, or 10–15 years. Almost overnight, and sometimes without any apparent warning, you find yourself standing in front of your son or daughter wondering what on Earth has happened! Your gorgeous boy or girl has transformed from a delightful child to a grumpy, sullen, moody, impulsive young adolescent who is actually answering back!

"Who are you?" you find yourself wondering or saying out loud, and at the same time reflecting on where you could have possibly gone wrong in your parenting. Take a breath – it is *not* the end of the world; it's just that your world and the world of your pre-adolescent are on slightly different angles, but all is not lost. An understanding of why these changes are occurring should ease your mind a little – but understanding the changes is one thing; *dealing* with them and still maintaining a positive relationship with your young adolescent son or daughter is the more difficult task.

I do not pretend to be a doctor or a child psychologist, so I'm not about to give detailed physiological or psychological background to all this. What I intend to do here is to put some of this background into context – if we don't know *why* our kids are changing, we can't possibly understand *how* we can cope with the changes on a daily basis. What we want, above all, is to know that our kids are OK...and that we are too!

What's happening to my child?

Middle years growth and development is massive. It is a period of great physical, emotional, social and cognitive development. While all this is going on, our kids are also leaving behind the familiarities of primary school and moving into the unknown world of secondary school.

Let's look briefly at just some of the changes your young adolescent experiences during this time.

Physical

Girls and boys experience the onset of puberty at different ages; for most girls it occurs around the age of ten, and for most boys around the age of twelve. Onset for girls can begin as early as seven or eight, and as early as nine years of age for boys – but this is not common. The entire process can take from one to six years and this process leads to *adolescence*.[1]

Adolescence itself is the transitional period between childhood and adulthood. Adolescents are no longer children, yet they are not miniature adults either. They are a special entity with special needs, and how we deal with them as parents can be somewhat tricky at times.

The physical changes are obvious in increasing height and weight, changed body shapes, increased body hair and developing secondary sex characteristics. Along with these obvious changes are the less physically obvious changes in hormones – affecting moods, co-ordination, self-image and relationships with friends and family...which leads us to the *emotional* changes experienced during this period.

Emotional

Dealing with the changes in emotions of young adolescents can feel like defusing a ticking bomb – one false move and you'll be hit by flying shrapnel! Some days are better than others and sometimes you just can't get it right. On those days, less is more – less talking, more listening...and more patience.

Surging hormones can take their toll on adolescent behaviour and moods and, while it is often difficult to deal with, it is a sign that the body is developing correctly. But not all mood swings and behaviour or attitude changes can be attributed to hormones. School or home-related factors can contribute to these changes...so don't just attribute everything to hormones; make sure you know what's going on.

If you keep in mind the kinds of questions our young teens are asking themselves during this time, you might understand why there are so many upswings and downturns in their mood and behaviour. It is obvious to your son or daughter that they are changing – they are growing up and out, and often they don't like it much.

Typically, they will start to question who they are; how they fit with family and friends; how others are perceiving them; what are they confident with and 'good at'. Because these questions are complex and the answers uncertain, the mood of teens can change quite quickly, and more often than not the frustrations will be vented on those closest to them – the ones with whom they feel safe and comfortable – *you*!

During these emotionally turbulent times, the best thing you as a parent can do is to:

- show love through communication and respect;
- provide support when they need it and ask for it – you need to be a little more subtle in your approach now;
- set limits – ground rules and structure are still important during this phase;
- not nag! Be inquisitive, but *not* interfering – inquisitions never end well.

Changes in the brain also affect emotions during adolescence, and this will be more clearly explained in the Cognitive section below.

Social

When our kids are young we work as a team – families operate differently, but basically we spend a lot of time together. Whether it's at the end of the working and school day, on weekends, during school holidays or the family holiday away camping – we all get to know each other well during those early years. We imagine it being like this forever, but we know it won't, and sometimes we're not ready for the change ourselves. So, when does it change? In general, when our kids enter adolescence.

TRUE TALES

I was driving my two boys home from school; they were six and seven years of age at the time. Adam, the seven-year-old, was relating a conversation he'd had during the day with a girl in his class. They were a bit sweet on each other.

"Mum, Jenny told me that when we get married I'll have to move out so that we can live in our own home. That's not right is it?" Adam was clearly well out of his comfort zone here and I could sense the panic!

"Well, that's generally what happens, Adam, but sometimes when people get married they stay with one of the families while they get themselves sorted with renting somewhere or maybe even a little longer while they save to buy a house." I was trying not to be too brutal.

"Ah, that's OK then," he replied. "I'm not staying with her family, I'm never leaving home. If Jenny wants to marry me, she'll have to live at my place. Ben can move out and she can have his room. If Ben doesn't want to move out, we'll have to get bunk beds and Jenny can sleep in my room, as long as I get to sleep on top!"

Oh, the innocence of the very young!

When they were six and seven years of age I couldn't imagine ever seeing my sons move out, and I didn't even want to think about it. Hopefully, as our kids grow up we provide them with a range of experiences which will give them the skills and the confidence to make sensible choices during the turbulent times of growing up...so that they *can* finally move out!

Peer groups are very important to our kids during adolescence. Many parents are confronted by the strength and power of the group and often saddened by what they feel is a sense of loss. In my experience this can be particularly so in single-parent families or single-child families.

The close bond between parent and child...more often mum and child... appears to be under threat. Suddenly your opinion doesn't count quite so much, and it seems that the opinion of the group nearly always wins. When parents speak to me about their concerns in this area I always remind them that if they have built a good relationship with their child over the years, they should have confidence in that. It might seem that they've lost them, but they haven't. They will, though, if they force them to choose or battle with them over priority.

The apparent dependence on peer groups and friends is all part of adolescent development – "Where do I fit?" is a very important issue for them. It doesn't need to be a 'them and us' battle; it may seem that what you think and what you say are no longer relevant, but you still need to maintain connection – you just need to connect a little differently.

We will be looking at the issue of making friends and establishing new social networks in secondary school in a later chapter; just know that you still have a very important role to play in your young adolescent's life. It doesn't stop when the pimples start!

Cognitive

Have you found yourself in the position of standing there, in front of your 13- or 14-year-old and asking – "Why did you do that? What on earth were you thinking?" If you haven't yet, you probably will. If you are lucky enough to receive a *verbal* response, instead of the more common grunt, shoulder shrug or eye roll, your treasure will probably say something like "I dunno" or "Whatever!" If you expect something more coherent than this, you will more than likely be very disappointed.

During adolescence, the brain is doing some amazing things – and, it seems, not always to the best advantage of your teen. We commonly refer to our brains as 'grey matter' and, put simply, it is the change occurring in the adolescent 'grey matter' which has a dramatic effect on their behaviour and their emotions. The grey matter is where all the nerve cells are and during adolescence there is about a 3 per cent loss in the frontal lobe. The frontal lobe is the area which controls impulses, forms judgements, plans and considers outcomes. It communicates with other areas of the brain through *synapses*, or connections between nerve cells.

At birth, each nerve cell (neuron) has about approximately 2,500 synapses (connections); by two years of age there are around 15,000 synapses per neuron. Up to the age of nine, the brain is twice as active as the brain of an adult. Around the age of twelve, the process called *synaptic pruning* starts to occur. The brain employs a use-it-or-lose-it principle and begins to prune or destroy the weakest connections. At the same time as this pruning is occurring another process called 'myelination' is also happening. While the brain is pruning away some connections, it is also strengthening and wrapping other connections with a white substance called myelin. The effect of this sheathing is to accelerate brain function by up to 100 times normal speed.[2]

The amygdala is an almond-shaped mass of nuclei found in the temporal lobe of the brain and is largely responsible for controlling emotions as well as deciding which memories are stored in the brain and where. Adolescents rely heavily on the amygdala when making decisions.

We can see by all this that the combination of pruning, myelin sheathing and reliance on the amygdala increases the chance of poor decision-making and risk-taking. It also means that our teens respond more on 'gut instinct' than reasoning and common sense – a very dangerous cocktail.

New findings show that the greatest changes to the parts of the brain that are responsible for functions such as self-control, judgement, emotions and organisation occur between puberty and adulthood.[3] This is good news for parents who are at their wits' end to understand some of the reckless and seemingly inexplicable behaviour of their young adolescent.

As parents, we can't stop the process of brain development and we can't stop our teens from making ill-judged decisions. What we need to do is provide plenty of opportunities for them to take safe risks and operate in a safe environment.

We know that if we allow our teens to ride around in a car with four other teens, we are placing them in an unsafe or high-risk situation and the decisions they make under these circumstances may well be disastrous. Don't cross your fingers and hope for the best – *you* are still the parent and you can say 'no'. It's all about how you communicate the 'no' and how you provide an alternative situation. Instead of hoping that five adolescents in a car get home safely, maybe allow the use of the car as long as there is only one passenger.

Parents often say that they tire of the arguments and the constant battles with their teens – don't give up! When speaking about brain development and its effect on adolescent behaviour, I often use the analogy of the 'terrible twos'.

If you have had a child who threw themselves on the floor of the supermarket when you refused to buy a toy or sweet they wanted, or if 'no' was the only word you ever heard from their sweet little mouth, think about how you handled that. Every parent has their own set of rules, their own set of limits, and when your rules were broken or your limits reached you used your own form of discipline to reinforce your expectations. Without limits, there is chaos and everyone is miserable. Imagine what your child would be like if you had ignored every form of unacceptable behaviour!

Now think about your teen. Keeping in mind that once synapses are destroyed they are never restored, we need to be vigilant in how we respond to the dopey decisions our teens will make. We might now understand *why* they behave as they do, but we don't need to *accept* it. If we fail to respond to unacceptable behaviour and fail to establish our own limits, we are potentially setting our teens up for a lifetime of dopey decisions and misery for the family – not to mention the increased risk to their safety and well-being.

'No' should still be a word in your parenting vocabulary – used in the right way with the right sentiment – and you may be surprised by the results.

TRUE TALES

Here is an example of how to get what you want by planting a few seeds – sometimes it works, sometimes you will have to resort to other means!

Our younger son wanted to go to a friend's party. All well and good, except that there would be no adult supervision – mum and dad had decided it would be a good idea to go away for the weekend! There would be a mixture of 17- and 18-year-olds there. The legal age for drinking in Australia is 18 and Ben was already just 18.

We weren't happy with Ben attending the party, despite the fact that he was a very sensible young man and legally allowed to drink. I could see that the party was a potential recipe for disaster and said as much to Ben. Of course, I received the response I expected: "Don't you trust me, Mum?" I assured him I did, but I wasn't too confident about the smooth running of the party without adult supervision. "Ben, there's no one there to make sure underage kids aren't drinking and there's no control over who comes and who goes. It's a nightmare waiting to happen. These things can get out of control very quickly, and if alcohol is involved it's very unsafe. We would prefer you not go."

You can imagine Ben's reaction. "Well, I'm 18, Mum. I guess you're just going to have to trust that if things go wrong I can look after myself. I'm sure it will be fine." At 18, it's difficult to say, "You're not going!" so I said, "In that case, Ben, we will be dropping you there and picking you up at 12." Midnight might sound late, but parties don't really get started these days till 10 pm!

Two days before the party Ben took me aside and said, "Mum, I've decided not to go to the party. There's heaps of kids going who I know will be looking for trouble. Justin [his best mate] reckons it'll be pretty horrible, so he's not going. I don't want the police showing up and ending up in jail!" I bit my tongue and replied, "Good decision, mate!" – better that than "That's what I said a week ago!"

Communication is the key here. How we communicate is very important in maintaining relationships with our young adolescents. We don't want to destroy years of positive relationship-building by setting battle lines now. Adolescence is a tricky stage for our kids and we need to be smart about how we handle delicate situations – confrontation won't work and an "I give up" attitude won't work either. We will be looking more closely at this issue of effective communication in Chapter 9 on 'attitude'.

LET'S SUM UP

In general, parents might find their young adolescents to be:

- less attentive;
- more assertive (even argumentative);

- more impulsive;
- more attention-seeking;
- more technically skilled;
- more connected to peers;
- more aware of what's happening in the world around them;
- more rights orientated;
- under more personal pressure;
- needing greater independence and challenge;
- needing learning to be more relevant and engaging;
- developing abstract thinking.

If you recognise all or some of these trends in your son or daughter, welcome to the real world...and you are not alone there. Be prepared for your young adolescent to test you and at times you will wonder which planet they inhabit.

Know the signs and consider how to work through the issues in ways that support your middle schooler, support your relationship with them and keep your family on an even keel.

Don't be soft, don't be hard...just right is the key. Hopefully, the information you have read here about the developmental changes of this particular group will give you a better perspective and a more positive outlook on how to handle your young adolescent. This is a stage like any other and information is power! So, power-up mums and dads – the fun is about to begin...and 'gorgeous' will return!

Chapter 2

Girls and boys – *vive la différence!*

It's not all about the obvious

We don't need a biology lesson on the differences between boys and girls – they're obvious. What is not so obvious is the wiring of the two genders and how these differences manifest themselves in the way our kids think, communicate, behave, respond and learn. As parents we sometimes wonder *why* our kids behave and respond the way they do...some insights into what's going on inside their heads might help.

Without delving too deeply into the physiology and neurology, it is important to know a little about the wiring of boys and girls if we are to give ourselves any chance of understanding, and dealing with, the complexities of their behaviour. Having said that, the argument over nature versus nurture is very strong in this discussion about boys' brains and girls' brains – just as there are differences *between* the genders, there are also differences *within* each gender. Experiences at home, at school and in the social context play a major role in determining future behaviour, skills and attitudes to specific learning tasks – we need to acknowledge differences and engage them.[1] But let's look at what we *do* know about the brain.

Boy brain, girl brain?

The *corpus callosum* is the bundle of nerve fibres that divides the cerebrum into left and right hemispheres. It connects the left and right brain and sends signals across both parts; it also transfers motor, sensory and cognitive information between the two hemispheres. By adolescence, the *corpus callosum* of girls is 25 per cent larger than that of boys, allowing for more signals to be sent across both hemispheres.[2] This helps to explain why girls are better at multi-tasking than boys...so we should stop giving our husbands and sons such a hard time for not being able to do more than one thing at a time!

At birth, boys are predominantly right brain oriented "with more cortical area devoted to spatial-mechanical functioning and half as much to verbal-emotive functioning".[3] What this means is that boys are generally better than girls at assembling jigsaws and puzzles, hand–eye co-ordination activities, visual–spatial tasks…and reading maps! Boys are wired to do.

Girls, on the other hand, are more left brain oriented at birth "with more cortical area devoted to verbal functioning".[4] This means that girls generally develop verbal skills more quickly than boys, as well as developing the ability to read and write earlier. Stronger neural connectors in girls enhance their listening skills as well as enabling them to detect tone of voice and interpret facial expressions more accurately. Girls are wired to talk – no surprises there!

Dr Leonard Sax, a highly qualified US psychologist and author of three books on gender differences and parenting boys and girls, claimed in a 2007 interview with Al Roker that boys are more interested in 'verbs' and girls are more interested in 'nouns'.[5] He suggests that the way our boys' brains are wired leads them to focus more on movement, while girls focus more on objects.

How does this help us to understand our kids?

Does appreciating these differences in our sons and daughters affect how we now view their behaviour? Should this insight alter our expectations of them, particularly during this transitional phase when their lives seems to be to hurtling through constant change? I must admit that, had I known all that I know now about what makes boys and girls tick during my early days of teaching, I would have been a better teacher. In hindsight, I probably wouldn't have changed the way I parented my boys…but I must admit to my patience being well and truly tested by their constant energy and their lack of apparent interest in anything I had to say beyond ten words…that hasn't changed!

US national educational consultant, Dr William L. McBride, made an extensive examination of the research to compile a list of brain-based genetic differences in girls and boys. I have included a short version here,[6] in the hope that it may spark your interest in pursuing more information. As I constantly say to parents, "The more you know…the more you want to know". Knowledge is a great source of comfort when we feel out of our depth. No one gave us a handbook on how to raise kids; and anyway, our kids are *our* kids and we need to spend time learning as much as we can about them as unique individuals – a few guidelines can't hurt!

Girls tend to:

- explain/describe feelings;
- multi-task;

- like eye contact;
- be more verbal-emotive;
- need encouragement to build self-esteem; feel uncomfortable under threat;
- be more critical of their performance;
- plan ahead.

Boys tend to:

- have difficulty explaining/describing feelings;
- single task;
- prefer limited eye contact;
- be more action-oriented;
- need challenge and relevance; feel challenged and excited under threat;
- over-estimate their own ability;
- procrastinate and be less organised.

Tying it all together

So, how can we convert this information into practical strategies we can use at home with our young adolescent sons and daughters?

To summarise boys, in very general and sweeping terms, we need to acknowledge that they thrive on activity (gross motor skills); don't like to talk much; don't like to make too much eye contact when speaking; can lose attention quite quickly if they are not interested or challenged (or if they can't hear!); are likely to take risks; can be impulsive; like to know rules and boundaries; appreciate consistency.

Girls, in very broad and sweeping terms, are effective communicators; focus on people, places and objects; develop the skills of reading, writing and drawing earlier than boys (fine motor skills); share thoughts and emotions more readily; can be anxious; have a tendency to internalise stress; are less impulsive; are able to multi-task.

When I mention these typical characteristics to groups of parents, there are always a few raised hands to refute these indicators. Brain research is constantly being renewed and reviewed and, as already mentioned, these are generalised indicators which may not always be obviously demonstrated by your son's or daughter's behaviour. My older son could read fluently by the age of five and his reading skills were far better than the majority of girls in his class. His teacher needed to supply him with more difficult texts to challenge him – reading just clicked for him at a very early age and he has always loved it. Ben, on the other hand, developed at the typical rate and was age-appropriate in his reading skills – yet I had read to them both equally and as frequently when they were of pre-school age.

More numerous than the parents who refute some of these indicators are those who state, often in sheer relief, that I have described their child 'to a tee'! More often than not it is the parents of boys who joyously claim to be revitalised and reassured that they have not failed in their parenting when their sons make impulsive decisions, won't talk, won't listen and can't sit still...it may be that he is a great kid just finding his way, and we need to guide him in the right directions.

TRUE TALES

I can remember a particular series of incidents which happened one day at school, many years ago, while I was on playground duty. I guess the reason I remember this particular duty is because the incidents so clearly highlighted the vast difference between boys and girls – at the time I didn't know why...now I do.

It was one of those duties when I seemed to be spending all my time breaking up disputes. It was probably one of those windy days when kids go wild! I was patrolling my area when I noticed a gathering – whenever this happens it's a good idea to scoot on over, as something is obviously drawing everyone's attention. I rushed over to discover two Year 4 boys, about nine or ten years of age, about to beat the living daylights out of each other. I moved in quickly to pull them off each other, took them to the side of the playground, shooed all the bystanders away and in my 'teacher voice' asked them what on earth the argument was about. Neither boy would look at me and neither would acknowledge with any more than a shoulder shrug. I demanded they look at me while I spoke to them and answer my questions, if they didn't want to be sent immediately to the principal's office.

In almost all of these kinds of cases, the 'recipient' speaks first: "He wouldn't take 'out' in the handball game," he blurted – still not looking directly at me. "Wasn't out," the 'perpetrator' replied. "Were too," was the retort. "Was not – so I hit him," responded the 'perpetrator'. Trying to contain my complete astonishment at the level of anger these two were feeling towards each other...over a simple handball game...I asked, "There must be something else going on here – want to tell me about it?" The 'recipient' spoke first – "Nah, that's it, just the handball game," at which the 'perpetrator' nodded in agreement. On the way to the office to complete a behaviour report on both boys, they were talking quite normally to each other about their soccer game the following Saturday! I was left to scratch my head in disbelief.

When I returned to the playground, I was greeted by two Year 3 girls complaining about one of their group who was being mean to one of the 'complainers'. "OK girls, let's go and sort this out," I said, hoping that the bell would ring to release me from my misery! By the time I reached the group, they were all over me, challenging me to give them a solution to their problem. Over the next five minutes I must have heard every detail of the three-year history of the relationship between these girls, and how it all led to this scenario! I could not believe the difference in the boys' and the girls' responses to sorting out an issue. The boys wanted to act on impulse and hit out, while the girls wanted to talk!

Had I known then what I know now, I might have taken the boys on a playground walk, walked beside them instead of confronting them head on and demanding they look at me, and asked a few more open-ended questions…more of a chat than an inquisition. Even though there didn't seem to be any more to it than a rush of blood and a desire for fair play, had there been more behind the incident I would have missed it. We need to keep these tactics in mind when dealing with our boys. Obviously, there wasn't too much bad blood between the boys, as they were quite happy to chat on their way to the office as though nothing had happened.

The girls, on the other hand, gave their miscreant friend the silent treatment for the next couple of days. Clearly, the strategies I offered the group for solving the problem failed and they dealt out their own form of punishment – isolation. Girls often seem to analyse these kinds of situation far more closely than boys, and come to a decision on action based on a blend of emotion and logic…and you have to hope that you're not on the receiving end of it!

LET'S SUM UP

- *Boys* can be more *physical, visual-spatial, impulsive, competitive and risk-taking.* They respond well to short time frames, clear and concise instructions, firm boundaries and fairness.

- *Girls* can be *more verbal, analytical, emotive and anxious*. They can describe their feelings, listen more attentively and for longer, are often less competitive with others and are low risk-takers.
- "There are no differences in what girls and boys *can* learn. But there are *big* differences in the best ways to teach them."[7]

Chapter 3

The new social network – real friends, not online!

New start…new friends

When I speak with Year 6 students in the throes of finishing their primary or elementary education, I often ask them this question: "What's the one thing you will miss the most about leaving this school?" I always ask the first person to shoot their hand up in the air, and my strike rate for this answer is about 95 per cent: "My friends" is the most frequently expressed answer. Similarly, when I ask, "What are you looking forward to most about starting secondary school?" the response is generally a mix of "new subjects" and "new friends".

Friendship and that feeling of belonging is a very powerful force. Young people often assess their personal value and worth on the quality of their friends, and the quantity. I have heard so many kids refer to a loner or an introvert as a 'loser' – absolutely not the case, but in their eyes this child who appears to have no, few or select friends is rated as a less than successful human being because they have a limited or non-existent circle of friends. This desire to 'fit in' is extremely strong among adolescents in transition to secondary school, but not nearly as strongly expressed among parents.

Research findings from a UK study[1] conducted in 2008 highlight some of the differences in the views of parents and their children on this issue of making friends and finding new friends at secondary school. While we are often more focused on how they will cope with the new demands of a different education system, different subjects, teachers, teaching styles and expectations – they are just wanting to feel part of it all; just wanting to fit in.

More than 500 children and families from six local authorities, or areas, across a variety of demographics were involved in this transition study.

When children involved in the study were asked what was the most important factor for them when considering which secondary school they wanted to attend, 40 per cent responded that staying with friends or siblings was the most important consideration; with parents quoting distance from home and school reputation for a high standard of teaching as being the top two responses (14.1 per cent and 13.7 per cent respectively).

Interestingly, when children were asked about their *concerns* about moving into secondary school, the number one response was "leaving behind old friends and teachers" (21.3 per cent); the number one response to reasons for *looking forward* to starting secondary school was "making new friends and meeting new people". A staggering 43.9 per cent of students listed this as the top priority, with the next highest rating to "more and interesting lessons, activities, clubs and facilities" at just 17.8 per cent. These figures and responses give us a real window into what is important to our kids in this transition phase – so don't underestimate it!

Parents, on the other hand, listed "bullying" as their number one concern about their child entering secondary school. This scored 53 per cent, with the next biggest concern being "safety" and "travel to school". Of the top eleven responses, "making new friends" ranked fifth and "sustaining friends" ranked eighth.

This study is one of many which offers similar insights into the views held by our young adolescents. We already know that kids in this age group are seeking independence, but at the same time looking to their peers for validation. Developing new friendships is a significant dimension of a successful transition, with the study claiming that "the more friendships, self-esteem and confidence children developed after transferring to secondary school, the more settled they were in their school life".[2] This is definitely something parents need to consider when assessing how well they think their child is settling in to secondary school.

Kids – "But I don't know anyone!"

It's tough for young teens juggling all the changes and expectations associated with starting secondary school – and even more difficult if they have left most of their friends behind. When a crowd of some 180 new Year 7 students rock up on the first day of secondary school and your son or daughter recognises only a handful of faces from their previous of school – none of whom were close friends – it can be a little daunting.

The cry of "I don't know anyone; how will I ever find new friends?" is common. If you recognise that your son or daughter might find it difficult to make themselves known to potential friends and a new group, then it might be worth considering these strategies to make that first contact:

- Have a short-term goal to *say* "hi" to at least one new person a day for the first two weeks – and *smile* as often as you can!
- Join *activities* at school that you either like or would like to try – sport, music, debating, choir, student representative council (SRC), etc. You have a better chance of meeting someone who has similar interests.
- Even if parents can drop you to school in the mornings and/or pick you up in the afternoons, think about taking *public transport* from time to time as well. This creates opportunities to meet other students who live in the same direction as you.
- Project the *image you want*! Be confident, positive and walk tall – even if you feel a little nervous…just *be yourself.*
- *Look out for other students* who might hang back a little – they might be looking for a conversation with someone new as well.
- Take along something a little *different* to school – this might be just a new style of lunchbox, a new phone app, etc. – which could turn out to be a real *conversation starter.*
- *Don't be an* "*I am…*", "*I have…*" or an "*I know…*" – this kind of introduction really sets the wrong tone and sends a message of superiority that doesn't go down too well with kids.
- Try to *remember the names* of the people you meet – it makes a good impression and shows you are interested in them.
- *Don't sit at the back* of the class all the time – try to sit in the middle of the room so that you can feel part of things.
- *Volunteer answers* in class – you are not expected to know everything, so if the answer is wrong at least you have given it a go, and others respect that. However, don't be the class clown in an attempt to draw attention to yourself – that's not the kind of attention you need!

TRUE TALES

Adam's first day of secondary school was difficult for everyone. He was nervous and so was I, as all of his close friends were scattered around a variety of secondary schools in the area.

Adam was not the most outgoing boy and he had chosen his school friends wisely from the start, and was very loyal to them. As parents we knew it would be difficult for him to settle in and find new friends at secondary school and Day 1 did not comfort us in the slightest. As his class group lined up single file, there was Adam – sitting at the end of the line, separated by at least two metres from the boy in front of him; his head was down and he was examining his fingernails, not wanting to make eye contact with anyone. For me, it was like watching him line up on his first day of 'big school' – heartbreaking.

It took some time for Adam to settle in, and I was always tuned in to listening for a name regularly mentioned which might signify a potential friend. Finally, about two weeks later, he mentioned a boy he had met in a class that day and said that they had 'hung out' at lunchtime as well. Yes!!!!

Without being too intrusive, I asked about his interests and Adam replied he played soccer. "He's playing next weekend at the field near us", remarked Adam. "Well, why don't you go up and watch him play and ask him back for a barbecue after his game. I can drop him home later", I suggested. The day panned out beautifully and Adam had found a mate. I was so glad I stepped in with a simple and casual suggestion that helped lay the foundation for a lasting friendship. Boys are often not as good as girls at creating these sorts of opportunities. Sometimes you need to nudge them along a little!

Adam's friend left secondary school at the end of Year 10 when he was 16, to pursue a trade, but the friendship remained strong despite his absence from school. He even joined the group on a trip to Fiji to celebrate the end of secondary school exams, and he and Adam are still good mates to this day – more than ten years after meeting in Year 7.

Parents – "Do we just stay out of it?"

It doesn't take too long for parents to realise that the 'rules of engagement' at the social level have well and truly changed by the time our kids hit secondary school. We are put back in our boxes very quickly if we overstep the mark in organising our kids to socialise with who *we* think might make good friends for them…and so we should. Now that we understand a little more about what makes our young teens tick, we should also realise that we need to give them enough space to find their way socially. Sometimes an opportunity, like the one mentioned in the previous story, will present itself…don't miss it!

During adolescence, the power of friendship is clear and undeniable. Whether we like it or not, our kids are entering a phase of 'separation' from us. They are looking to find their own identity, and this developing identity will be strongly linked to their friends and peer group.

Secondary school for many kids will bring a fresh start, a new opportunity to create a new circle of friends and a new identity...and we don't always like the friends our kids choose. We can't just sit back and watch our kids self-destruct, but we need to handle the whole friendship issue much more delicately than we probably did when they were younger.

'The wrong crowd'

Parents are terrified of their kids associating with 'the wrong crowd'. In my experience of working with parents, they might not rank finding new friends as a top priority concern when their son or daughter enters secondary school, but they *do* worry about their kids getting together with peers who they consider to be the wrong 'kind' of friends.

We are very blinkered when it comes to our kids – and sometimes a little too quick to label other people's children as the trouble-makers. When parents say to me, "It's not my child; it's the kids they hang out with who are the problem", I sometimes wonder if the parent of another child in that group is making the same complaint about this parent's child!

The bottom line is, our adolescents will associate with those who make them feel comfortable and accepted – they *choose* these friends, so we just need to accept the fact that we don't see what they see. However, this is not to say that we turn away from potential trouble and throw our hands up and say, "Well, I guess they'll learn the hard way" or, even worse, "I told you this would happen". On the one hand, we want to maintain a good relationship with our teens and keep them safe, but on the other hand we need to let them grow up and make mistakes along the way – including making possibly not the best choices in friends! So, how do we do both?

These are a few tips which might just save the day in terms of keeping your relationship with your new secondary schooler intact, as well as sending the message that while their choice of friends does not change the way you feel about them, you are not about to completely step out of the loop.

- *Don't overdo the criticism* of their friends – it sounds like a broken record and your kids will switch off...as well as argue against you and defend their friends. Remember that friendship ties are strong and your adolescent's identity is linked to their friends...so when you criticise their friends, you are also criticising them.
- Try to *separate the behaviour from the individual* – instead of saying something like "Your friends are trouble-makers", better to say "Your

friends seem to make bad choices and find themselves in trouble – I worry that you will be in trouble too". You are not labelling the adolescent, but rather the behaviour – and hopefully your teen will see you are genuinely concerned for their welfare and not just interested in criticising their friends.

- While your kids are making choices, you still have the right to do the same – if the behaviour of your adolescent is affected by their friends, and their subsequent behaviour is unacceptable by your standards, apply *consequences*. Accepting *responsibility and accountability* for actions are all part of growing up.

- *Set limits on time* spent in social settings with their friends. Particularly in the early days of secondary school, parents still feel they have a level of control over where their kids go, with whom and for how long. If clear expectations and boundaries are established early, parents are less likely to have as many arguments over social outings. The level of mutual respect and understanding established early can avoid repeated conflict later. There may still be rebellion – but it may be diffused a little more easily.

Child behavioural therapist, and creator of the Total Transformation Program, James Lehman, claims that "while your goal as a parent is to keep your child protected and safe, your child's goal is to be with people who like him".[3] It seems the message here is that the more we criticise and rail against our adolescents' friends, the more likely we are to push them *towards* their friends rather than away from them.

LET'S SUM UP

- The transition to secondary school coincides with a period of adolescent self-discovery and identity; *friends are closely linked to this developing identity*.
- Our kids will be drawn to friends with *similar interests and similar attitudes*.
- Be *supportive* of new friends – but keep eyes and ears open for any problems.
- If there are problems *tackle the issues, not the individual*.
- Your secondary schooler needs to remember that the best way to find good friends is to *be yourself*!

Chapter 4

Parents keeping a connection with their school

"My baby's all grown up…"

That first day of secondary school is tough…for everyone! Just as the first day of 'big school' brings with it a barrel-full of mixed emotions, so too does the first day of secondary school. Of course, the kids don't display their nerves too much – that wouldn't be cool – and we, as parents, don't have to prise our children from our legs when the morning bell rings as we did when they were five. However, there is definitely a strong scent of uncertainty in the air…and there are plenty of mums wearing sunglasses despite the overcast skies! As we make our way home we might find ourselves thinking, "My baby's all grown up – where do I fit in now?"

"…and it's all different now"

Parents are generally very involved with their primary schools – either by way of parent committees, fund-raising, canteen support or more directly supporting teachers in the classroom. So, what happens now?

TRUE TALES

A couple of years ago I came across a young woman I hadn't seen for years. She told me she had a son who was finishing his final year of primary school. There was just the two of them – a single mum doing a great job providing for her son, and she was clearly very proud of him.

I asked whether or not her son was looking forward to high school and she replied, "Yeah, *he* is…but I'm not." "Why not?" I asked. "Because that's when I'll lose him." I asked why she thought that way and she said, with a hint of sadness in her eyes, "Well, he'll want to be with his mates more, and I left school early so I don't know anything about high schools now – I can't help him like I could in primary school."

I don't know how well I did at convincing her in the five minutes we had that she still had a lot to offer both her son and her school – it's hard when confidence is low and uncertainty is high…but there *are* ways.

Finding the 'right fit'

The dynamics of secondary school are certainly quite different, and for many parents somewhat overwhelming – even threatening. Parents seem to have the impression that high schools would prefer less contact rather than more…if there's a problem, they'll let you know. In addition to this, their kids are giving very strong signs that they want to cut the apron strings. It's not that they mind seeing you at school, you just need to be a little more selective in your reasons for being there. I have even had parents tell me that when it is necessary for them to visit the school for a particular reason, they have been warned not to acknowledge their son or daughter if they cross paths – "It's not that I'm ashamed of you, Mum, it's just not cool to have your parents at school."

Having said this, strong parent–school partnerships have been found to have a positive impact on student engagement and achievement, and not just at the primary school level. Not only do students achieve better, but they also stay at school longer.[1] There have been several studies over recent years which have concluded that parental engagement *in* the classrooms, with parents sharing knowledge and expertise in areas such as home economics, woodwork, etc. has had a very positive impact on student engagement…and the kids actually *like* it!

A study conducted in the UK in 2008 explored the effect of parental engagement in their children's learning, with a focus on technology. A key finding indicated that "home–school communication is seen to be essential in fostering parental involvement and engagement".[2] So, can we really afford to switch off once our kids make the move from primary to secondary education? Evidence strongly suggests that we should *not*!

So, how do we keep positive connections with our children's new secondary school? Some parents find this easier to achieve than others. Many parents have told me that their past, personal experiences in education have prevented them from being directly involved with their children's school, even at the primary level. Once their children move on to high school, they are even less inclined to connect with the school. They feel embarrassed, frustrated and inadequate and often totally out of the loop in terms of what's going on at school. I ask these parents if there were a way to connect with confidence to their children's school, would they? The answer is overwhelmingly 'yes'.

Involvement vs engagement – are they the same?

In my experience, the vast majority of parents want the best for their children – they sometimes feel that their kids head off to high school each day and enter a vacuum until 3 pm…and they would like to know more about what is happening in that vacuum.

TRUE TALES

This is quite a disturbing tale and, sadly, an all too familiar one in the world of schools and parenting today.

I was conducting one of my parent workshops in an inner-city suburb and it had all the signs of being a tough gig. In the main, the parents fell into that category of 'hard to reach' or 'disengaged' parents – not because they didn't love their kids, but because their own educational experiences had not been happy or positive ones and they felt ill-equipped to help their kids now entering the turmoils of both adolescence *and* secondary school.

The session started slowly and the body language and demeanour of the group was a little on the chilly side – I had a feeling that perhaps they considered me to be an outsider coming in and telling them how to be better parents; or perhaps the situation highlighted their feelings of educational inadequacy.

I started with a few jokes about my own personal frustrations with adolescent boys, as I had *two* at the time, which helped them to see that I was actually a real person – a mum possibly experiencing the same frustrations they were. Suddenly, they started to open up and share.

There was one mum in the group whose story has stayed with me to this day – not for being extraordinary, but for being what is probably more commonplace than not. She started by telling me that she had a son already in Year 8 and one in Year 5 – not yet ready for secondary school, with one more year to go in primary, but her concern for him was already evident.

Her older son was a chronic truant and had changed schools three times in two years. I asked why, to which she replied, "I only want what's best for him. He said he couldn't make friends at his first school, so we changed. Then he said he didn't like the teachers and they didn't like him...so we changed again. He obviously doesn't like this new school because he's only been to school five times this term. The school rings me to ask where he is and I don't know because he goes off in his uniform every day. I'm sure they've given up on me and I guess they think I'm just a bad parent."

When I asked what kind of relationship she had with her school, she admitted to being very reluctant to visit, despite the school's numerous requests, because she didn't really know what she should say. She had disciplined her son but it wasn't working and now she was worried that her younger son would follow in his older brother's footsteps – "He's already skipped school a few times and says if it's OK for his brother, it's OK for him. I want to do something now before it's too late – I just don't know what. I just want be a good mum."

Her comments reminded me of so many staffroom conversations regarding parents who had been judged to be missing the mark in their parenting skills. If we know the answer, or an avenue where help can be accessed, we assume that everyone else should too...or if they don't know they will just ask! Wrong! Sometimes parents are simply too afraid to ask, for any number of reasons, and the end result can be disastrous. This mum obviously wanted the best for her boys.

Fortunately, schools are becoming increasingly more engaging and alert to the needs of their families and are providing ways and means for parents not only to connect with their school, but also to access support. Schools are not that scary – make the first move and you may be surprised by the results.

How to 'connect' with your school

The capacity of parents to connect with their school, particularly their secondary school, is very much dependent on the willingness of the school to include parents as an integral part of the school's operation. There is also a

very big difference between parent *involvement* and parent *engagement*…
and fortunately there is an increasing trend among schools to build stronger, more engaged connections with their parents.

Parent 'involvement' refers to the variety of ways in which parents support their child's school. Assisting with canteen duties; covering books in the library; fund-raising; parent committees; voluntary work around the school, etc. are all common and structured ways in which parents have supported their schools in the past…"What can I *do* for my *school*?" rather than "How can I support my child's education?"

Parent 'engagement', on the other hand, refers to a much deeper level of *connectedness* with their child's education. Parents and teachers working *together* to achieve mutually agreed goals is *real* parent engagement…who knows your child better than you? But for many parents – and schools – this is a tough goal to achieve. The opportunity to directly assist at the primary level is much easier – helping with Maths or reading groups, supporting school choir practice or coaching the netball or soccer teams. Secondary school is different.

'Engagement' does not imply that we should begin to question the professional knowledge and insights of teachers; but it does suggest that we, as parents, can make a huge difference to our children's education if we are more switched on to what is happening in that vacuum…and, more importantly, that we take a more proactive role in supporting what is happening at school and continuing this supporting influence at home.

As mentioned earlier, this proactive role in secondary education is largely dependent on the school's philosophy to genuinely engage parents, as well as the parent's level of confidence to actually assume a stronger partnership. We also need to keep in mind that sometimes our kids don't want us to have a high profile at school. So, how do we juggle our kid's needs with our own needs, the needs of the school and any barriers which might prevent us from establishing a good relationship with our school?

Are there any barriers to connecting with your school?

Schools are communities, and just like any community there are differences and special needs which should be addressed and met. Families are diverse and needs are varied, and sometimes this can present a challenge both to schools wanting to engage their families and families wanting to feel valued by their school.

What are some of these barriers?

- Lack of understanding of how the new system works – "Who do I ask about…?"
- Staff in secondary school don't seem to be as accessible as in primary school – move from one classroom teacher and a home base to many different subject teachers.
- Misunderstanding of parents' role – by parents themselves and sometimes by the school as well.
- Lack of confidence – parents' past experiences with school may affect how they contribute now.
- Disability – parents need to be able to access the school safely.
- Literacy/learning difficulties – parents may have difficulty completing forms, reading newsletters, communicating clearly with the school, etc.
- Cultural and language differences – parents lack confidence to become involved with the school and may feel excluded.
- Parents working – unable to attend functions, meetings, etc. in school hours.
- Childcare – difficulty accessing suitable childcare for younger siblings so parents can participate in school functions.
- Communication from school to home – needs to be direct, transparent and written clearly; limited use of educational jargon which is unfamiliar to most parents.

"*What can I do if I want to connect with my school, but can't?*"

If you can relate to any of the barriers mentioned…or indeed if there are others I haven't mentioned which affect you, it is really important for you to alert the school or a friend you trust to act on your behalf.

Making first contact with your new school may be difficult for you, but if you can access as much information as possible about the secondary school your son or daughter will be attending for the next six years it will make a huge difference to your relationship not only with your school, but also with your young adolescent.

Seek out parent representatives who are actively involved in the school – these may be parent advisory board members, parent committee members or community liaison officers who work closely with school staff, parents and the wider community to promote effective partnerships and networks. If language is a barrier, access the help of a translator to make contact with the school.

There are any number of ways to make that first move and some of the tips below might help.

Let's get the ball rolling...

If your school encourages a deeper level of connection with their parent community, other than the traditional fund-raising and physical support, here are some tips to break the ice:

- Make contact with your school – if you don't feel comfortable actually going to the school, perhaps make a phone call and leave a message for your child's year co-ordinator, or email the school.
- Familiarise yourself with the subjects and names of subject teachers – ask your son or daughter what they are enjoying and whose classes they enjoy – ask casual, open-ended questions...not the Spanish Inquisition!
- If there are parent training or parent information sessions available, make sure you attend. Perhaps arrange to meet someone there so you don't have to go in alone.
- If there is a parent room (or parent 'hub') at your school, make a visit one day to see what goes on. This is an ideal opportunity for you to meet other parents. Ideally your parent room should be equipped with tea/coffee facilities as well as a range of information on external support services, such as community health, language programmes, social services, etc.
- Check your child's newsletter regularly (either hard copy or on the school website) to find out if there is a parent group within the school – either parent committee or school advisory board. Make a note of the committee members and contact them if you are unsure of anything and would prefer to speak with a parent as first point of contact.
- If the school requests parent expertise to support teachers in subjects such as food technology, woodworking, computers, art, etc. – volunteer! Research shows that this kind of parent engagement, particularly at the high school level, has had a huge impact on student engagement – the kids actually *like* seeing their parents in this role at school, even secondary school!

There is no 'one answer fits all' on the issue of keeping a positive connection with your school, especially secondary school. Probably one of the best, and most subtle, ways you as a parent can maintain a connection with your school and, more importantly, a connection with your teen is by recognising and utilising your life experiences.

Over the past several years I have worked with families from vastly different backgrounds and circumstances. A common trend, however, is for parents to take a big step back once their kids leave the primary school nest. We have already acknowledged that this is a difficult time for kids and also for parents..."What do I know about how secondary schools work now? It's so long since I went to school...everything has changed!" Does this sound familiar? If it does, welcome to the world of parenting today.

"Do I have any skills to help my teen at school?"

Convincing parents that they have more to offer their young teens than they realise is not always an easy task. However, if you have ever had a job, ever had to complete a task by a certain time or ever had to prioritise a list of things to do...you *can* help your teen!

The skills we use as parents in our everyday lives are both transferable and relevant to school. When I speak with parents about how they can keep that connection with their kids in secondary school, I remind them of the common practices they have utilised, if not perfected, over time. The skills of planning, multi-tasking, prioritising, delegating, etc. are just as relevant to your child's learning as they are to any career.

Instead of saying: "Don't ask me...it's all different now, and I can't help you", *step up* and say "I can do that. I'll show you how I tackle something like that in my job." It doesn't matter that you have never studied History; it doesn't matter that you hate writing essays; it doesn't matter that you don't understand the Maths – what matters is that you *want* to help your child and support their learning and study...and your life experience can be invaluable.

If you say "I would like to help, but I don't know how", you are probably sending a message of defeat to your kids. Your support is *not* dependent on your own personal level of learning or achievement – it is very much dependent on finding a way in, on sharing life experience and skills... keeping a connection.

Our kids will generally give us a chance, particularly in early secondary school, but if we don't seize the opportunity then the window can close very quickly. Once the window closes and our adolescents access help somewhere else, it can be very difficult to re-open.

When parents confide in me that once their child enters secondary education, they feel powerless to help and are quite happy to take a back seat... "because my child tells me to butt out!"...I ask them exactly what has changed so significantly in their adolescent between the end of primary school and the beginning of secondary school?

In the case of Australian schools, there is a *5-week* break over the Christmas/New Year period before a new school year begins in late January or early February. Do you really think your child has grown up and matured so much in five weeks that you can afford to take your eye off the ball? Given this perspective, parents generally acknowledge that they need to remain in the loop – they just need to be more subtle!

You may well be asking the question, "How can we be engaged, connected and still up to speed with what's going on...and be subtle at the same time?" Skills you have gained over a lifetime come in very handy when dealing with young teens. We will be looking at how we can utilise these skills to maintain the connection with our sons' and daughters' school and education in subsequent chapters.

LET'S SUM UP ⟩

To keep a connection with your son or daughter as they move from primary education to the next level you need to:

- Keep an *open mind* about the change – don't shut the door because you're afraid you might say the wrong thing!
- Establish *early contact with the school and staff* – if you don't want to visit the school at first, make contact via email or the phone to introduce yourself.
- Make sure you *inform* the school about any particular issues which you feel might affect how, when or why the school communicates with you or your child.
- Try to make informal *contact with other parents* if possible – this might smooth the introduction process.
- Check the *school newsletters* regularly so that you feel up to date on what's happening at the school and in the classroom.
- Share your *life experiences* with your child – don't feel you should know everything! You have more experience and skills than you realise; these life skills are transferable to school.
- *Confide...don't confront!* Communicate and work *with* your teen rather than over-organise or step back – if they make mistakes, hopefully they will learn by them!

Chapter 5

Aligning the stars – finding that balance between work and play

Then…and now

How school life has changed!

I remember my school days being a mix of fun, friends, learning and strict rules – but fairly stress free. We rarely went on excursions; in fact, I don't remember an excursion until secondary school. In most Australian primary schools back then we did have tests and I do remember having to study for them!

We had limited homework and plenty of time to play after school, and I don't remember my parents ever being asked to attend parent/teacher interviews. We played, we learned, we read; our parents were not invited to be involved directly in our education, as that was left to the teachers. Parents were informed of our progress at the end of the year, with a set of exam or test marks to prove it and a 'position in class', along with some basic comments on a report to round it off. Then on to the next year. The only time a parent visited the school – primary or secondary – was to sort out an issue…and then playground gossip was rife!

So, what about now? How has our system changed and how have these changes impacted on parents? We all know how much harder kids work in school now – after more than 20 years as a teacher I have seen the enormous changes with my own eyes. I don't always like what I see. Our kids are under increased pressure to perform, and gone are the days when a kindergarten teacher could just let the kids have a sleep because it was too hot to do anything after lunch. As curriculum demands have increased, time-out in class has decreased.

After having endured two consecutive Higher School Certificate final year exams with my sons, I can safely say our kids are under pressure. Having said that, I firmly believe that there is a lot to be said for exposing our kids to a little pressure – whether we like it or not, life is riddled with it and they have to learn how to cope. School is as good a place as any to start.

What *is* 'balance'?

The dictionary will define 'balance' as 'a state of equilibrium'…some parents would define it as 'compromise', 'negotiation' or (more often than not) 'nagging a teenager'.

Finding just that right blend of work and play is tough – and not many adults can lay claim to a great deal of success with this one. In this fast-paced world we generally feel time-poor, over-worked (often underpaid), stressed…and we haven't even started dealing with our teens yet.

On the one hand we, as parents, may feel burdened by the stresses of work and live in the hope that one day our lottery numbers will come up and we can have the life we *really* want!

On the other hand, as our kids progress through secondary school, we often find ourselves at loggerheads with them because *their* life balance swings very much in the opposite direction. The secret to surviving stress and coping with the increased demands of school is the ability to strike that *balance* – it's a *life* skill, not just a skill for secondary school.

The 'ingredients' of balance

As I see it, there are a number of ingredients which, when combined in the correct measure, can promote a sense of well-being and life balance. No doubt you will be able to add a few extra ingredients of your own – whatever works for you and your family.

These are my top five:

1   healthy lifestyle
2   communication
3   choices
4   routine
5   goals.

Healthy lifestyle

We all know the drill – healthy diet, regular exercise, plenty of sleep. But we *are* talking about teenagers here!

It may be overstating it a little, but I think most parents would agree that a healthy diet for many teens (particularly developing boys, who have the ability to consume their dinner before yours is even on the plate) probably does not match *our* understanding of a healthy diet.

They will quite happily exist on fast food and takeaways or – if they are feeling that they need to eat healthy for a change – might even pick up a sandwich. Not that there's anything wrong with fast food in moderation… but have you ever seen your 180 cm 16-year-old son go for the healthy takeaway option?

A friend of mine has a teenage son who won't eat anything green – obviously severely limiting his choice of healthy foods. Funny thing is, he doesn't have a problem with eating the lettuce out of a burger…or green jelly beans!

Diet has become a more hotly debated issue these days, especially in light of the alarming statistics relating to obesity on the one hand, and body image and eating disorders on the other.

These issues need to be addressed quite separately from our general overview here; however, one point needs to be made: the brain is a very powerful machine and, like any machine, it needs to be treated well…and fuelled. Diets which encourage the reduction or elimination of carbohydrates (particularly complex carbohydrates) are denying our brain the opportunity to function at its best.

The brain requires fuel in the form of glucose to receive, process and retain information. So, a healthy bowl of pasta, brown rice, muesli or oats might just be *one* way to support your teen's learning.

Another major issue we have with our teens is their apparent lack of the need to sleep. For a variety of reasons they are staying up later…and sleeping in later as well. Of course, sleeping in is a major cause of arguments on school days. We know the story: mum beating on 15-year-old's door with:

- "You need to be up – NOW!"
- "You'll be late for school!"
- "The bus will go without you!"
- "I'm not dropping you off again, I was late for work yesterday!"
- "Your sister is already waiting at the door!"
- "You don't have time for breakfast!"
- "I'm banning the computer for a week! "
- "I'm banning Facebook! "
- "I'm confiscating your mobile! "

…any of these sound familiar? Before we give up entirely, we need to consider a couple of interesting factors which might explain these sleep patterns – and, no, it's not just to annoy us.

Research now suggests that, during the teen years, the circadian rhythm – or body clock – resets. It has been suggested that this change in rhythm is due to melatonin (brain hormone) being produced later at night for teens than it is for adults and children. This activity makes it more difficult for teens to feel sleepy at what we, as parents, would consider to be a normal time.[1]

The unfortunate side-effect of late nights, but required early starts on school mornings, is that our kids are constantly sleep deprived. Regardless of the change to their body clocks, they still need eight to ten hours' sleep every night...and *everyone* in the household suffers if they don't get it!

More important to note, however, is the fact that it is during sleep time that our brains consolidate and store information learned during the day. We are filing and preserving information...so it makes sense to say that the less we sleep, the less we have filed away for future use.

But for those parents who wage a daily battle against the teen who refuses to go to bed at a reasonable hour, these few tips might help:

- Try to establish a *regular bedtime* from the onset of adolescence (I would say to my boys – "If you can't sleep, at least you're resting your eyes!").
- *Avoid caffeinated drinks* at night.
- *Exercise* regularly – but not shortly before bedtime, as exercise then acts as a stimulant rather than a relaxant.
- *Avoid stimulants* such as long phone conversations, computer or electronic games, MSN/Facebook chats just before bedtime – if they need to set aside time for 'social networking' come to an agreement on a time frame.
- Read, study, etc. in *natural light* if possible – bright, fluorescent light stimulates the brain rather than relaxes it.
- Create a positive *sleeping environment* – mild temperature, darkened room, limited outside noise, etc.
- *Wake up to bright light* – open curtains, lights on if necessary – this lets the brain know that it's "up and at 'em" time...even if the teen response to this is a little less appropriate!

Communication

If you follow the principle that being on the outside looking in is better than not looking anywhere at all, you are probably setting yourself up for communication to be limited to *what* your young adolescent wants to talk about, and *when*. You might be waiting a while! It's a dangerous practice to sit back and wait, and you are potentially sending the wrong message to your teen.

Admittedly, secondary schools do have a tendency to send the message that you need to hand over more control to your kids now that they are growing up, and I think parents often interpret this message to mean, "If there's a problem, we'll tell you; if not, keep away." Secondary schools certainly encourage more responsibility from students in terms of their learning and their actions – but they are *not* discouraging parental communication between school and home.

After more than 20 years on the inside of schools, I can vouch for the philosophy that more is better. When dealing with children, particularly adolescents who are undergoing enormous physical, intellectual, social, academic and emotional growth during these secondary school years, for teaching staff to have inside knowledge of what is happening in their world outside school can be enormously beneficial.

Parents need to keep the lines of communication with their schools well and truly open – there's nothing more soul-destroying than mishandling a situation with a student because you don't have all the facts. We have no hesitation in bringing important information to the notice of staff at primary school – we need to continue this practice in secondary school. Obviously, we need to use a more subtle approach – the one thing teens hate is for mum to trot up to the school and sort out their problems!

On the home front communication is vitally important, too. Our middle years kids, those from 10–15 years of age, tend to be more impulsive, more defiant, more in need of peers, more attention-seeking, more opinionated, more independent...and less attentive! This means that while *we* are trying to guard them against risk-taking and erratic decisions – *they often aren't listening!*

A friend once told me, "If you can't say to a teen what you want to say in ten words or less, forget it!" I have never been able to say what I want to say in ten words – not just to a teen...to anyone. Just ask my boys! Once you see the adolescent eye roll, head shake, monosyllabic grunt, muffled words spoken too softly for you to hear – you know you have gone *way* past ten words. I have experienced a combination of these responses many times.

One thing I have learned through parenting and teaching is that the secret to communication is humour – not always easy in some situations, but so much more effective. Mutual trust is built over time, and even when it seems our kids have turned into almost unrecognisable aliens, rest assured they will resurface at some stage...if we keep talking *with* them, not *at* them!

Sorting through issues together as a family, with humour thrown in if possible, is far better than a lecture. Don't be afraid to tell your kids about your own mistakes – the long-term after-effect can be amazing. This is a personal experience I shared with my boys when my older son, who was then in Year 7, was having some problems with a friend who was constantly copying his work.

TRUE TALES

"I was in Year 9, attending an all-girls school. We were a group of five, with one a fringe-dweller – we all got along OK, but she didn't quite fit in. Her mum worked at the school. This girl was well-liked by teachers and was a very nice person herself. She was not a very confident student and, in hindsight, she possibly felt pressure to achieve because her mum was there.

She often asked for our help with class work and we didn't refuse; however, copying in class tests was becoming an issue so we decided to 'set her up' – not the best option, but probably typical of 15-year-old girls' decision-making.

I made it easy for her to her copy my answers and sacrificed a couple of marks by deliberately writing the wrong answers down – of course, she made the same mistakes. When the tests were returned – with her answers and marks identical to mine – we decided to confront her and accused her of cheating…which we thought was obvious. Tears flowed, she told her mum and claimed bullying and false accusations, and I was hauled into the principal's office. I was placed on detention and absolutely humiliated. To this day I do not know what went on behind closed doors, but both student and mum left the school."

When I related this story, and explained that I had been a student leader and popular with teachers and students, my boys were horrified. Mum was human, she made mistakes…and she was even a bit mean! We used this story to discuss what might have been better options – talk to a teacher, ask mum or dad what might be the right and better thing to do, etc. The secret is finding golden opportunities to share yourself with your teen – it beats a lecture any day.

Adam sorted out his problem in his own way, and far better than I did!

Communication is probably the most important key in the developing relationship we have with our children – and critical in this mixed-up world of adolescent development. The old adage "It's not what we say, it's how we say it" is so true. Words spoken in haste and frustration can lead to regret; just as well-considered and encouraging words can lead to increased trust and understanding. *How* we communicate can greatly affect not only the attitude of our teen, but also our attitude towards them. We will be exploring this issue further in Chapter 9 on 'attitude'.

Choices and routine

When speaking with parents, a common belief seems to be that a busy child is a child less likely to get into trouble. Up to a point, this is true – however, we tend to over-stimulate our kids, organising every minute of every day to avoid the dreaded cry "I'm bored!" I do remember a time when holidays provided us with great opportunities to use our imagination.

My dad was in the army, and for the first five years of my life I lived in an army house in the army barracks. Nothing too fancy about army barracks I can tell you – the memories are still vivid, and it was a refreshingly simple life. Mum would steer me and my sister outside into the 'fresh air' to play. There we would be in the middle of the backyard, one tree in the corner, yard surrounded by a leaning, timber paling fence…and nothing else. Between us, we would invent new games, chase each other, play hide-and-seek, and Mum would spend a lot of time playing with us and reading stories. We were not allowed to watch more than an hour of television before bed and, of course, there was nothing like computers, electronic games or mobile phones to while away our time. We made our own fun.

When we talk about finding a balance between work and play, we still seem intent on the 'play', or leisure time, being structured in some way. If our kids aren't learning at school or studying, they're playing organised sport, learning a musical instrument, being tutored, taking dance lessons, etc. Of course, there's nothing wrong with these activities, except that their very nature requires organisation to get there on time, pick up and drop off siblings to other activities, and entails late dinners, early dinners, dropping friends home, taking homework in the car to complete while waiting for a sibling to finish their 'leisure time' activity. All sounds a bit too hard!

If we find ourselves constantly telling our children that they need to be more organised with their homework, think about how difficult that is when they are out after school almost every afternoon of the week. If we want our kids to develop *effective homework and study routines*, we need to give them the opportunity to establish some kind of regular structure to their week.

Students who operate on an overcrowded schedule of after-school activities, and constantly leave work to the last minute, will struggle to meet the demands of secondary school. As parents, we need to say 'no' and encourage our kids to start making some sensible *choices* – for them as well as for us.

A couple of stories I think are worth sharing here in terms of guiding our teens towards finding the right balance. We have more influence and control when our kids are in primary school, but it is a slightly different story in secondary school.

Once we've compromised on the number of after-school commitments in their early secondary school years, we need to continue to monitor their welfare as they progress through the years ahead.

TRUE TALES

A girl I met some years ago was in her final year at school. She was an exceptional student with a strong desire to follow a path in Science. She dedicated her time to study and exam preparation, leaving little time for anything else. Her Higher School Certificate results were outstanding, and good enough to earn her a scholarship to study Science at university – she was *so* excited! She managed to find herself a part-time job to earn a little pocket money before university started and thoroughly enjoyed the break from study.

Some months passed before I saw Anna again, and the first question I asked her was how she had settled in to uni life and was she enjoying her course. I was shocked to hear that she had left uni after only three weeks. I asked her why, and she answered: "I just couldn't concentrate. I would sit in lectures and then wake up halfway through the lecture to realise that I hadn't heard a thing. I couldn't concentrate, I had no motivation and I just didn't care." So, I asked her what were her plans for the rest of the year, to which she replied, "I have deferred my scholarship and am taking leave. I plan to get a job, earn some money and clear my head. I'll go back next year." She did not return the following year.

Instead, Anna worked. She lost the desire to study, seemed to lose her passion for Science...and, to my knowledge, has not returned to study. Anna may well have made the right choice for her at the time, but it seems such a pity to see someone with so much potential lose the desire to follow through on that potential.

A more balanced approach to study may well have avoided the 'burn out' that we so often see in the senior years at school – and this 'burn out' is starting even earlier in our young ones.

TRUE TALES

This story about Lisa presents the flip-side to the whole balance issue...

Lisa was a sports fanatic – she swam, she ran, she played ball sports. She trained almost every afternoon for *something* – whether for her swimming squad or as a member of both netball and basketball representative teams. Sometimes she went from one sport to the other in the same day.

I first met Lisa when she was in Year 7. We would chat about a variety of things – often her interest in sport and her wish to make sport her life in some capacity when she left school. She had little or no interest in school, despite the fact that she was quite a bright student.

By the end of Year 8 she was still completely focused on her sport. I asked how she managed to fit everything in – school, homework, social life *and* her multiple sporting commitments. She said she didn't care too much about school and she always finished her assignments at the last minute, and didn't care too much about the marks because she hadn't put a lot of effort in anyway. She was passing, so she was happy with that. I wondered then how she would survive beyond Year 8, when the workload increased and the intensity raised.

Two years later, I came across her mum. "How's Lisa?", I asked.

"Not well", was the reply. I asked what the problem was and was absolutely horrified to discover that Lisa was under the care of a counsellor. Lisa was now in Year 10 and heading towards sitting major exams – all the kids were panicking, including her. She wasn't performing well in assignments and tests and fretted over the outcome of upcoming exams.

When her mum saw the writing on the wall at the beginning of the year, they agreed to pull the plug on her sporting activities – in the

> hope that giving her more time to finish work and study for exams might reduce the pressure. It helped a little – but because she had never really developed a *balanced routine*, not only wasn't she coping, but she also had no sport to release her energy.
>
> Probably the saddest part of this story from my perspective was the fact that this young girl, at 16, was not only struggling to find her way, but she required the short-term use of medication to help her. Her mum was surprised to discover that her daughter was not the only one in this position. One of Lisa's friends had said to her "Life is just too hard" – at 16!
>
> This seems to be a clear case of balance having swung far too much in the other direction – but the end result can be the same.

It is very difficult to look into the crystal ball with any degree of certainty – and hindsight can be very cruel – but we need to keep trying to negotiate and re-negotiate best interests with our teens. We need to support *life balance*.

Goals

There is one thing that will keep us on track – goals.

Whether we realise it or not, we are constantly setting goals – might be as simple as getting the final draft to the boss by the end of the day, ticking off the 'to do' list of chores you want to finish at home or it might be (as I have so often experienced with students) remembering to pack your lunch to take to school!

This is a significant topic – so you will find more information and details about the importance of short- and long-term goals and SMART goals in Chapter 12.

LET'S SUM UP

- Keep an eye on what they *eat* and how much they *sleep* – and when.
- *Communication* – yes, we need to be clever in *how* we get our message across at *home* (and avoid World War III), but we also need

to maintain a connection with their *school*. We can't always assume that all messages will filter back home on their own.

- Life is all about *choices* – your kids can't do *everything*. As a parent, you still have the right (and responsibility) to say 'no' to multiple activities – the art of compromise is a skill.
- Keep your eye on the ball for *study overload* or *activity overload* – they can both have a very negative impact on your teen.
- Develop a *routine of work and play* as soon as possible – a little bit of unstructured relaxation is good for the soul.
- *Goals* – give your teen direction – but make sure the goals are *theirs*, *not yours*!

Chapter 6

Work environment – basic or brilliant?

Is there a 'one size fits all' solution?

We're all different. What might work for you in terms of the ideal work environment might not work for your adolescent – so don't push it!

The ideal work space is generally one that suits the personality and learning style of the student. Your teen may be the kind of person who thrives on working and studying in a room that is cluttered with all their favourite things; others like lots of colour; others like a little background music (sorry…it should be classical, not head-banging!) to stimulate the senses; others like a more clinical environment where they feel they can't be distracted by too much hype around them. The sooner your adolescent finds what suits them, the more likely they are to settle into a routine of work and study.

We will be looking at learning styles in more detail in Chapter 11, but it should be mentioned here that *how* your teen learns (their learning style) also affects how they study and work most effectively, and their work environment at home should reflect that. For example, if your teen is a visual learner, you might expect to find lots of sticky notes plastered all over the door and walls in their room, as well as highlighted notes – visual cues are very important for these learners.

If your teen is an auditory learner, you might expect to hear them talking to themselves while memorising facts and information, as repetition aloud promotes effective learning for these students; they may also like to bring other students into their work environment for group or paired study. This is not a trick…it actually works for auditory learners.

If your teen is a kinaesthetic, or hands-on, learner then it may be that they need to keep a supply of gum handy as chewing gum has been shown to assist kinaesthetic learners to concentrate; they may also have a supply of stress balls (or 'squishy' balls) in their room – not to alleviate stress, but the constant squeezing of a soft ball, the clicking or twirling of a pen or having something in their hand while studying actually aids concentration – kinaesthetic learning is all about being on the move and using the body while learning and studying.

Are there some 'basics' to an ideal work space?

Yes! Regardless of specific needs or preferences, there are *some* features of an ideal work space that suit all.

Here are a few suggestions to turn your 'basic' work space into 'brilliant':

- lighting
- heating and cooling
- work area
- storage
- distractions.

Lighting

Adequate lighting is a priority in developing a 'brilliant' work space. Intensity and direction are critical to the level of productivity and quality of your teen's work.

The lighting itself doesn't need to be brilliant, with natural light being the best choice. Of course, homework and study are generally night-time activities, so which kind of lighting is best?

A study, conducted in 1999 by the Heschong Mahone Group,[1] concluded that daylighting had a direct effect on student performance and concentration. Natural daylight emits a continuous spectrum of all light wavelengths, so when we are choosing the best lighting for a study area we need to consider what is closest to natural daylight. Full spectrum lighting is considered to be the best for study for these reasons:

- it is gentle on the eyes, allowing you to work and concentrate for increased periods of time, avoiding headaches or eye-strain;
- it offers the full spectrum of colour, which is the way we see in natural daylight;
- it enables you to see details more clearly;
- it is energy-saving;
- it emits less heat.

A range of full spectrum globes and complete lamps, lights, etc. is available – just check with your nearest lighting specialist to find the most appropriate choice for your home and study area.

Heating and cooling

This is a little like the three bears. What we're looking for is not too hot…
not too cold…just right!

If your adolescent is studying or working in an environment that is too
hot and stuffy, the result is lethargy and the tendency to nod off to sleep
(though your adolescent might tell you the nodding off is due to the 'boring
assignment'). If the work area is too cold, they are likely to be thinking
more about how uncomfortable they are than focusing on the task in front
of them.

So, how do we achieve 'just right'? It's pretty simple really. Ideally, the
work area should have access to fresh air coming from an external source – a
cross current of air is also fine. Natural ventilation is always best. Of course,
this depends on *where* in the world you live!

However, if the area where your adolescent will be spending most of their
time working and studying is not near a window, then a door leading out to
a balcony or porch works too; alternatively, the use of fans is another option
– although these tend just to circulate existing air. Air conditioners come in
handy…as long as you don't leave them on for hours; just long enough to cool
the area down for as long as you need to be there.

If we are looking to warm the room rather than cool it, it's never a good
idea to leave a heater on full blast or long term. Warm the room, then turn the
heater off. Closing the door can make the room stuffy very quickly, but if closing the door aids concentration and separates your teen from distractions
happening elsewhere in the home, then have a window open just enough to
allow the flow of fresh air…and put on more clothes!

Work area

Now we've sorted the lighting and ventilation, what are we looking for
when setting up a 'brilliant' work space?

Parents whose children are just entering secondary school often express
their concern that their child has never really had a designated space where
they can do their homework. They have more than one child sharing a
room and this has never really been a problem in the primary years because
study and the need for independent work has not been an issue.

Homework up to this point has been short-term, generally taking no longer than 45 minutes to an hour per school night, and there has been no need
to study for exams. So, their concern is to find a place where their child can
concentrate and have all their essentials close at hand…but how do we do
that when kids need to share a room?

Let's look first at the ingredients for a well-balanced and effective work area, assuming that our student has his or her own room. Use these suggestions as starting points for modifications if your son or daughter is sharing a room with a sibling, or if you prefer to move them away from their bedroom into a more open area for work and study purposes.

We have already covered *lighting* and *ventilation* and a general overview of workspace. Let's look at some specific requirements in relation to other key aspects of study space, as well as storage and distractions:

- A *clear, flat area* on which to work – whether a desk is in your teen's room or in a different area, it is a good idea to separate work and rest areas. That means no homework or study on the bed! There is plenty of evidence to support the notion that the brain associates bed with rest and sleeping...not problem solving or remembering facts and figures. If your teen wants to remain alert, that is far less likely to happen if he or she is lying or lounging on the bed.

- As well as working on a flat, clear area your teen should also be seated in a *comfortable (but not too comfortable) chair*. The chair can be adjustable, but the seat needs to be flat and the back of the seat supportive. You can purchase an ergonomic chair if you like...but it's not necessary as long as you maintain good posture and have the computer positioned correctly, with the monitor at eye-level.

- *Clutter-free space* – there's nothing more soul-destroying and de-motivating than to look at the area where you are about to continue your assignment or start to study for an upcoming test...and be unable to see the top of the desk! What I strongly suggest is that they have some kind of system that enables them to manage the junk which can pile up very rapidly. Bookshelves, tubs or containers for books and stationery; expandable files for loose sheets; and a pen holder for all their writing utensils – all simple but effective ways to de-clutter. Another practical tip: suggest they pack up and tidy their work area each day to avoid wasting time trying to find what they used yesterday and can't find today because of all the mess – spending time looking for things does not encourage the best frame of mind for work and may lead to increased procrastination and then a total lack of interest in even making a start.

- *Storage* – we will be covering this in more detail in Chapter 7 on organisation, but I would like to affirm the claim that having a system of filing and storage is absolutely essential for secondary school. This could be a system of coloured and labelled folders, expandable files, filing cabinets, lever-arch folders with multiple subject divisions – whatever suits your teen, and that you know they will use. Keep it simple, practical and not too fancy.

Despite the fact that, in this era of electronic everything, students are less inclined to use paper, they may still need to download some of their research and final essays, and assignments may still need to be submitted as hard copy. Without an adequate system of storage they will find it difficult to keep on top of the paper trail, so start good habits early.

- *A quiet and distraction-free work space* – this can be a tall order in a home where there are several siblings and a constant buzz of conversations and noise. While you may not be able to control all distractions – there are some which you can. A situation where social network sites like MSN, Facebook and Twitter are open while your teen is attempting to concentrate on the job has 'disaster' written all over it. Every time they respond to a message that pops up in front of them increases their chance of completely losing track of what they should be doing. I know they will say that they can do it...they claim to be great at multi-tasking – "Just because you're old and you can't do it doesn't mean I can't" is a fairly typical retort from your teen. Multi-task...yes they *can*; multi-task *well* and retain focus...all evidence suggests *very unlikely*!

Think about negotiating time for social networking as separate from study/homework time – there's nothing wrong with reaching a com-promise and, once you have reached an agreement, stick to it. If they break the treaty, have a suitable consequence in place. I have been told by many parents (who were initially convinced that that it wouldn't work) that their negotiations have proved very successful and not only has the level of work achieved in a given time improved, but the relationship between parent and adolescent has also improved. It is certainly worth a try.

- *Music* – many students work best under noise-free conditions, but many other students with whom I've worked claim they simply can't focus without there being some kind of low-level noise...others claim that not-so-low-level also works (sorry...no way!). There seems to be mixed messages on this issue, but the strongest evidence suggests that certain kinds of music actually stimulates memory and retention, while others inhibit and distract.

Research suggests that music with a pattern of 60 beats per minute actually aids concentration and that classical (especially Baroque) music is the best by which to work and study.[2] It has been shown to slow the heart rate, increase relaxation and stimulate learning and memory function. Unfortunately for our young ones, contemporary music (in general) runs at 100–140 beats per minute. This beat pattern actually lowers the brain's ability to retain information. I often suggest to parents that the traditional relaxation music (the sounds of the rainforest, etc.) that we have tucked away, given to us by a well-meaning friend or therapist anxious for us to re-establish a state of calm, should be passed on to our kids. We don't have time to be relaxed – we're too stressed about our kids! Music works for some and not for others...but if your teen insists on background music while studying, keep it low, keep it classical and keep it lyric-free.

TRUE TALES

A few years ago I was asked to deliver a brief version of my transition to secondary school workshop to a group of incoming Year 7 parents, as part of the school's orientation evening. I must admit to being a little underwhelmed by the prospect of delivering a rapid-fire 45 minutes' worth of information to an already information-overloaded audience. I had been part of audiences like this when my boys started their secondary school journey and I couldn't wait for everyone to stop talking! I felt like standing up and screaming, "Enough! I'm tired, I'm anxious and I won't remember all this by the time I have done all the Christmas shopping and we have had a holiday break!" I'm sure you can relate to this.

So...how to maximise the information, minimise the time...and make people laugh at the same time? There were obviously a few issues I could not eliminate, and the subject of organisation and preparing an area for study and homework was one *not* to be deleted.

I whipped through the suggestions and the demonstrations, asked if there were any questions, related a few home truths about my home-front battles with my two boys...and moved on. At the end of the mini talkfest, bleary eyed parents stumbled out to their cars and I was left to wonder if I had touched anyone at all in the audience.

Two months later, after our five-week summer break and two weeks into the new school year, I was asked to return. This time my role was a little different, as this was to be a simple follow-up session – an informal and social get-together of the new Year 7 parents.

As were heading down the stairs to make our way to the library for refreshments, a mum approached me. "Aren't you the lady who spoke to us last year about how to help our kids be more organised and settled for secondary school?" she asked. "Yes, that's me," I replied, hoping I wasn't about to be in trouble for something I had said...or not said.

"I'm so glad you're here," she continued. "My son has a learning difficulty and I was so worried about how he would cope this year. The advice you gave about work space and organisation was the best advice I've ever been given – wish I'd heard it when my two older kids started. The day after I'd heard your suggestions, I took my son aside and said, 'We're going to get on top of high school before you even start!' We bought all the folders and organised his room before the holidays finished. He came home from school earlier this week and said, 'Mum, I have my first English assignment and I know just where I need to file it.'"

As this mother continued to tell her story, I noticed a few tears beginning to well. "You have no idea how my son's enthusiasm and confidence made me feel. For the first time in his life he feels in control – I just hope it lasts!"

I must admit to having a few tears welling myself, and it was then that I realised that it doesn't matter how small the steps are, as long as we take them. The small step of setting your adolescent up in a work area that makes them happy is such a positive start. Small steps sometimes equal great progress!

LET'S SUM UP

- Your teen's work area must suit them – *environment* to match *needs*.
- *Lighting, ventilation, clear and uncluttered work space, seating, storage* and *limited distractions* are essential elements of a 'brilliant' work area.
- *Negotiate social networking* usage with your teen – set some ground rules.
- *Pick your battles* – your needs may differ from your teen's needs. If they are working where they feel comfortable and 'switched on', monitor their progress and, if it works, go with it!

Chapter 7

"Where's my assignment?" – the need to be organised

One of the most challenging tasks for students moving into secondary school is setting up an organisation system that works. They are moving from a very nurtured and regulated system to one that requires more responsibility and independence. The bottom line is – they need to be able to keep control of their 'stuff'! I've seen students in their senior years still scrambling to find that assignment, those notes, that text book – and it isn't pretty. The sooner they feel in control, the better they will function in secondary school.

So, smile if one of these comments reflects your fairly regularly expressed frustrations:

- "I don't know where it is...the last place you left it!"
- "I'm not your slave. If *you* had put it back where it belongs, you wouldn't have lost it!"
- "You have an assignment due tomorrow...and you can't find it?"
- "It's probably in your room somewhere – good luck with that one!"

...and probably our most frequent and over-used rant, "You need to be more organised!"

If you haven't smiled at least once, you obviously don't live with teenagers...or you have been blessed with exceptional fortune, and possibly should consider some form of 'cloning' of these rare creatures...you would make a fortune!

The reality is that most teens are not terribly organised, nor have they any real or immediate desire to change – it's often up to us to force the issue...if we want to survive and avoid unnecessary conflict. Of course, it is more difficult to confront and remedy the situation if we have our own issues with organisation.

The life of a primary student

With a background of more than twenty years in primary classrooms, it is easy to see *how* our kids can find themselves in a world of organised chaos...and how they might get away with it in primary school. In secondary school, the lack of a system becomes a very real and frustrating problem – for students *and* parents.

Imagine this scenario in a fairly typical Year 5 or 6 classroom...and welcome to *my* world! Thirty gorgeous boys and girls, all eager to get started on the day ahead, entering the room with backpacks ready to be unpacked for the day. Lunch orders in one hand, late notes in the other, book club money in one pocket and a signed excursion permission note hanging out of another one. Lunch orders in the basket, late note on my desk, book club money in the tray and signed excursion permission note, again, placed on my desk.

Now, while I'm sifting and sorting through all the bits and pieces on my desk, checking that lunch orders have been placed in the basket, reminding that excursion notes need to be in *tomorrow*, these little treasures are unloading everything else into either a tote tray, which had been labelled very beautifully at the beginning of the year, or an under-desk. *Everything* lives in the tray or under-desk for an entire year.

At the end of each term I insist that we clean out our trays – and it is simply amazing to see the condition of that left-over sandwich, or the 'thing' that was formerly an unwanted banana. The cries of "Ah...that's the newsletter Mum couldn't find a month ago" or "I knew I had put my savings book somewhere!" fill the room – it's like a treasure hunt!

The life of our primary children is a very nurtured one. As teachers we keep close guard over regularly needed workbooks and all the important stuff. They are often stored on shelves somewhere in the classroom and distributed by our ever-helpful classroom student helpers when required. These books are then collected and returned to their home on the shelf, ready for next time. Returned work, homework tasks, reading books, diaries, etc. are kept by the students...filed lovingly in the depths of the tray or under-desk. So, what happens when a loose sheet of paper – it might be a writing assessment task – is returned? Unfortunately, and often after *hours* of careful marking, it is filed in the bin on the student's return journey to his or her desk – or shoved into the abyss of the under-desk or tray.

Now, what happens when these youngsters enter secondary school? Alarm bells ring...no under-desk, no tote tray, only a locker. "What will I do with all my stuff?"

...and secondary school?

So, what *does* happen in secondary school? Believe it or not this is what our kids think...

TRUE TALES

Recently I visited a primary school to work with the Year 6 students in preparation for high school. It was a lovely school and the kids were great. Parents had been invited to come along and the session was held in the classroom, with all 40 Year 6 students attending and a handful of parents sitting at the back.

We had already covered a few topics and the kids were very open about their concerns for what might lie ahead in secondary school. It struck me that sometimes we underestimate the importance our young ones can place on issues that we, as adults, might consider trivial – but which to them are major concerns.

The issue of *organisation* was next on our hit-list of topics and we chatted quite comfortably about exactly how we store and file our everyday work at primary school. I mentioned that in secondary school they would most likely be given a locker which would need a security lock. Mayhem ensued..."What happens if I lose the key?"; "What happens if I can't *use* the key?"; "What happens if I forget which locker is mine?" It's a *locker*...with a *key*! But to 11-year-olds, this is major change...and we mustn't underestimate its importance.

Now to Blake and Jessica. After we had overcome the locker hurdle, we began to talk about what to do with those "bits of paper teachers keep giving you". The 'bits of paper' generally refer to assignments, homework or research tasks. Keep in mind the fact that many schools now upload current assignments and tasks onto their intranet – however, at some point students will need a hard copy for reference. So, I pulled a piece of paper from a folder and focused my view on the boy in the front desk. I asked him his name and continued:

"Blake, I have given you your first assignment in History and it's not due for another three weeks. You only have a locker which you can't use until recess, and you have no under-desk or tote tray. What will you do with this piece of paper?"

Without flinching, hesitating or batting an eyelid, Blake fired back, "I'll probably lose it!"

After the laughter died down and parents clapped in open agreement that this is exactly what would happen, a small hand shot up from the middle of the room. A classmate, Jessica, obviously felt she had an answer to Blake's apparent acceptance of defeat. I looked her way and asked her what she would do.

"That's easy. We have diaries. I'll put it inside the cover of the diary," she chirped.

"Excellent idea, Jessica," I responded, "however, what happens when you have three more assignments you need to fold and store inside the cover of your diary?" I added.

Jessica looked at me for a moment and replied, "I guess I'll have a pretty fat diary, and I probably won't remember what I have in there." Fair comment. "Are you likely to remember which assignment comes first, Jessica?" I asked. "Probably not," Jessica sighed, "and I usually forget to take my diary home anyway!"

Ah…organisation! The world is full of Blakes and Jessicas – and not *all* of them are 11 years old.

It is true that most schools now have a very comprehensive intranet, which students access via the school portal and their own log-in. Current work commitments are uploaded and students can monitor what is due and when. This can overcome the issue of the lost assignment; however, students generally need a hard copy at some point…it is so much easier *not* to lose it in the first place than to be forced to download it from the school intranet!

Tearing your hair out yet?

I must admit that I am a creature of systems and order – I just can't function in mess. I do like to think I am reasonably normal, however, as I have encountered some who not only label every item in their pantry, but also order everything according to size! I have bent my own rules over time… because I live in a world of men!

My husband, an engineer by profession, can be meticulous over details, but not so much over where he may have last placed his keys, sunglasses, wallet, screwdriver, secateurs, sun block…anything, really.

Our two boys – both now gorgeous young men and still living at home – seem to have developed their father's liking for the question, "Any idea where my...is?" This question is *always* asked in my direction, as I appear to have unwittingly earned the title "the gatekeeper".

In their younger years, our older son Adam, would know where everything lived – quite taken by the view that everything had its rightful place. Even his slippers would be carefully lined up, right next to each other and placed at the foot of his bed. Meanwhile, younger brother, Ben, had perfected the laissez-faire attitude (i.e. wherever it falls is where it stays). I always wondered how two children, only 13 months apart in age, and having the same parents, could be *so* different!

As time progressed, the gap between Adam's fastidious nature and Ben's, shall we say, casual nature began to lessen. Right through the primary years Adam maintained his system (with Mum applauding his every move) and Ben maintained his 'she'll be right' flair. However, once we hit secondary school a whole new monster emerged.

Adam, as the first to experience secondary school, felt a little overwhelmed by the whole experience and his very ordered world hurtled in other directions. He needed to store and file notes, make summaries of topics studied, keep returned assignments instead of throwing them away as was his custom in primary school and learn a whole new system of study and revision. We tackled one obstacle at a time – a very smart move for those whose children have difficulty coping with change. We got through it, Adam developed a new system, and his world regained its balance.

Ben, on the other hand, was a much more difficult customer. In terms of his ability to cope with change – his resilience – he was a star. In terms of his filing, storage and organisation in general, he was a meteor crashing to Earth! In his very first week at school he lost his entire sports uniform. He left it on the train – sports shoes and all – but sadly did not even remember that he had lost it until I asked him to put his washing in the basket – at 7pm that night.

The following week he made sure he remembered to return home with his *new* sports gear intact – but left his jumper on the train instead, "because the train was stuffy and I got hot!" My first attempt to cure his disorganised state of mind was to visit the second-hand clothing pool at school and buy him the biggest, least attractive and least expensive replacement jumper I could find – he did not dare to lose this very unstylish replacement and it remained with him right through until the end of Year 12 – when it, at last, fitted his 180 cm frame!

Despite both boys differing markedly in personality, both struggled with the endless 'paper trail'. We found a system that worked for Adam and, while he did have his ups and downs, he seemed to know where most things were...most of the time.

Ben took absolutely no notice of my constant suggestions (he would say 'naggings') to become more organised and in control. I struggled for the first four years of high school, hearing every possible reason to justify his lack of organisation. My 'light bulb moment' happened when he was in Year 10.

TRUE TALES

Picture the scene – family sitting at the breakfast table. Four people focused on the day ahead; teenage boys inhaling anything and everything that remotely resembled food; father talking about his plans for the day; mother certain she has forgotten something, but determined to finish that piece of toast before she again checks her list. Sounds familiar?

While munching on what is now half a slice of toast, son Ben saunters over to the fridge and opens the door. "Mum – you said you got more Vegemite. It's not here."

"It's there, Ben – in the fridge," says a calm (for now) Mum.

"No, it's not, Mum," retorts Ben.

"Yes it is, Ben. Have you looked?" replies Mum, with slightly clenched teeth.

"Mum – fridge door…open…looking," is the response – offered in that style that only a teen can use effectively.

"It's on the second shelf, Ben – I can see it from here!" says Mum, with slightly elevated blood pressure.

"Ohhhhhh. What's it doing there? It's usually on the top shelf next to the margarine and the marmalade!"

It was at this point that the lightning bolt struck. If a 16-year-old boy can't find something he wants to *eat*, what chance is there of him finding something he doesn't want to *do*…like an assignment…without a system?

So, we had 'the talk' and I suggested that if he wanted to survive his final two years of senior school – both academically and without me taking to him with a cattle prod – he would need to get his act together. He did…and we all survived – no cattle prod necessary!

What works? S.O.S. for parents

When I speak with parents, I remind them that it doesn't matter how much *you* know, how much your son or daughter knows you are trying to help *them*, how frustrated they might be by constantly wasting time trying to find that assignment or those study notes for an exam tomorrow, or how much money you spend on fancy filing systems with everything that opens and shuts – the bottom line is that they need to *want* to change.

Adolescents are not yet wired in to the same priorities as us, and their brains are still making connections – we cannot give up on them, we just need to be patient.

To summarise: this is what worked for us – keep in mind that there is no 'one size fits all' solution, but having a starting point is better than nothing.

This very simple system of folders is one I suggest as a starting point for organising assignments, notes, completed tasks, etc.

- *Four labelled folders* – for *each subject* requiring research or assignments or long-term tasks.

  1 *One display folder* – this folder is where the assignment is placed as soon as they bring it home, assuming they remember to remove it from their bag!
  2 *One document wallet* – to store all the information needed for the assignment. This might be downloaded material from the internet or handwritten notes from school – anything that is required to complete the task. This wallet can be cleaned out after the assignment is finished and notes recycled.
  3 *One coloured plastic wallet* (or something similar) – to store any notes from the assignment which the student feels might come in handy for study or revision.
  4 *One manilla folder* (or something similar) – for storing returned tasks/exams, etc. in that subject for revision purposes.

- *Colour code* each set of folders (e.g. *History* might be *blue*).
- *Magazine holders* – to store these folders in an upright collection so that students can easily move their 'stuff' from one place to another.
- *Calendar* or *wall planner* – part of being organised is knowing what's due and when. They will be provided with a school diary, but a more visual approach, like having a wall planner or calendar with all commitments entered and on display takes the heat off everyone in the family.

You don't need all the fancy bells and whistles – kids really like to keep it simple. Experience of dealing with thousands of families suggests that if it's not simple, they won't use it!

LET'S SUM UP

- *Be proactive* in your advice – don't tell them what not to do – offer *positive advice.*
- Be *patient! Developing brains* don't always respond in the way we would like.
- What might seem trivial to you may be a concern for your teen – *listen* to what they say.
- *Plan a system* that works for everyone...especially your son or daughter.
- *Folders* and *storage files* – a good place to start!

Chapter 8

Managing time – it can be done!

Blowing the lid on bad habits

If you haven't already heard yourself spit this one out…you will, one day. As sure as night follows day, at some point at least one of your children will cause the elevated blood pressure, the increased heart rate, the flushed face, the shrill tone and then, finally, that age-old question that no child in my experience has ever satisfactorily answered…"Why do you *always* leave everything to the last minute?" I often wonder what exactly it is that we expect our little treasure to say. Maybe it's "Well, I really enjoy putting myself under enormous pressure" or "I want to see how badly I can fail" or, more likely, "Just to annoy you!" Well, tick that box because annoyance doesn't even come close to the frustration and helplessness we feel when we know our kids are setting themselves up to fail.

   If you are the same, always leaving everything to the last minute, you probably haven't given your child the best start, or set the best example – but it's never too late to change old habits. Recognising a fault and acknowledging the need for change is the first, big step towards a more productive and less stressed life – it's amazing how much better we feel about a job, a task or an assignment once we decide to make a start.

Is *time* really the enemy…or is it you?

Time management is a skill and, just as other skills need to be taught and refined, so does this one. For some, staying on top of commitments and work comes easily, for others procrastination rears its ugly head and spoils any chance we may have of achieving our best results. Secondary school is all about multi-tasking and juggling more than one assignment at a time. If you have followed the advice in Chapter 7 on organisation and have a copy of a planner somewhere visible so that you can see upcoming due dates for work, you are off to a good start to teach your new secondary schooler the skills involved in managing workload.

How many times have you asked your son or daughter, "When are you going to make a start on that assignment you've been putting off?" If you never need to ask this question, you are very rare indeed and your children are super motivated. More commonly, parents *often* ask this question and for some it's *all the time!* So...what can we do to turn our nagging into encouragement so that our kids will commit to getting the job done?

No matter how organised we might be, there's always that task we don't want to do, that job we leave at the bottom of the pile. If we are guilty of procrastination ourselves, then it's pretty easy to spot in our kids.

We all tend to delay starting the tasks we least enjoy...the ones that we know are going to be time consuming and hold limited interest for us. We often choose to do what we like first and act on the less interesting tasks later. So, at times we have some choice in the tasks we delay. However, our kids are constantly faced with assignments they don't want to do – not too many kids rush home to make a start on a History or Geography assignment.

Nagging our kids is *not* the solution – it just adds to family stress and emotional outbursts which, in the long run, are counter-productive. Some parents opt for the easier (but unwise long-term) solution of actually *doing* major sections of the assignment because they are tired of nagging and think that if they start the ball rolling their kids can finish the work on time – big mistake! All that these parents are doing is fostering a lack of responsibility, encouraging laziness, stifling initiative, reducing their child's opportunity to feel a sense of achievement when the job is done...or risk failure if it's not done...and simply not letting them stand on their own two feet.

No parent wants to see their child struggle and fail; if we can see that our kids are really putting the effort in and still struggling, of course we will help; but let's not strip them of the opportunity to find out what they're doing right and what they need to change.

"Where do I start?"

A critical factor in avoiding procrastination is developing a system...a plan of attack. There is no one-size-fits-all, but *any* size is better than none! Here are a few points for students to consider as a basic plan to avoid procrastination:

- Take the assignment out of your bag and read it!
- While you are reading through the task, highlight the important words to give you a sense of what you have been asked to do. Target key

words, like 'describe', 'analyse' or 'explain' – any words which help to explain the task.

- Redefine the task – summarise, in your own words, the requirements of the task. By doing this, you have made a connection with the assignment, gained a basic understanding and established a starting point for research and planning.

- Use a planner or timetable to jot down a few time slots for work – allocate time for research, drafting, editing, etc. Once you have broken down the assignment into chunks, it is easier to see how progress can be made; rather than looking at an assignment as a huge slab of boring work that you have no interest in completing.

If you stick to specific and achievable time frames or chunks, it's a really nice feeling to tick off the sections you have completed...you can see that progress is being made.

If your son or daughter makes a commitment to *do* rather than *delay*, they may be surprised at how much more positive they start to feel about school and their learning. The feeling of being in control and on top of the workload is critical to student attitude and success, especially as they move into the senior years of school.

As a parent, this kind of planning is no doubt part of your everyday world...it needs to be part of your teen's world as well. So, rather than doing the assignment for them, steer them towards developing essential life skills they can practise and refine for life-time use...and then you can stop nagging!

"Is it ever too late to get my act together?"

The short answer is 'no'. Of course, old and bad habits are hard to break, and the earlier you start guiding rather than nagging, the better the results – academically and emotionally.

TRUE TALES

After years of school, then study and finally teaching, I knew how important it was to have a system and how easily we can slide into denial and procrastination. I also knew that I had two very different sons, one more organised and self-motivated than the other. As boys are not often the easiest to organise, I had to get in early with, let's say, 'encouraging' time management routines and systems. I figured if I started *before* they hit the adolescent eye-roll and "whatever, Mum" stage, I might have a chance!

Homework reached its peak of around an hour a day in Year 6, and both boys had homework contracts – a Monday to Monday list of tasks to complete, which included reading, spelling, writing tasks, maths and research. The nightly spelling and maths were easy to control, but the research tasks were a little trickier. I would ask them which sections of the research they thought would take the most time and then we would allocate some time slots throughout the week to get it done.

They soon began to realise that if they didn't want to be doing all the research over the weekend when they should be outside having fun with their mates, then they had to commit to small amounts of time spread across the week. They developed a routine and a habit, a good one, which helped to keep their heads above water right through secondary school and into tertiary study.

There should be no need for the massive panic and stress that plagues senior secondary school students. The common whinge "I had to stay up all night last night to get that essay finished" says more about a student's lack of management than commitment to a task.

Time management tools

We can spend an enormous amount of time and money on all the bells and whistles – electronic diaries, planners and organisers; a variety of apps for your laptop or mobile phone; things that beep at you to remind you where you should be and why…stop already! If you have a teen who you *know* will struggle with managing their time effectively in secondary school, the tried and true KISS (Keep It Simple, Stupid!) principle works just fine.

Let's start with the basics. Here are a few ideas:

- weekly, monthly or term planners
- calendars
- diaries
- 'to do' lists
- checklists.

Whether your teen chooses one or a combination of time management tools, the important point to remember is that the key use for these tools is planning and prioritising – skills your child has not needed to master in primary school, but will need to tackle and master in secondary school.

Planners

If neither you nor your child has used planners before, it might be a good idea to start with the basic weekly planner. The following offers a simple, but effective, way to use a weekly planner:

- Pencil in all the extra-curricular activities for that week first (e.g. Monday 4–5 pm – tennis coaching; Thursday 5–6.30 pm – tutoring, etc.)
- Think about what schoolwork needs to be completed throughout that week. Allocate time slots on free days in order of priority – some tasks may need more than one time slot. Don't leave it all till the night before it's due!
- When researching, allocate time slots of 30–45 minutes – most of us have trouble maintaining concentration and distraction-free focus on one topic for longer than that.

If you are thinking about monthly or term planners, the same principles for use apply. The added advantage to using a monthly or term planner is that you can start to plan ahead more effectively. Assignments tend to come in waves or cycles, based on teacher marking, assessment and reporting cycles.

It's a good idea to mark in due dates for all tasks, as well as dates for exams or topic tests – that way you can plan your study ahead, as well as juggling time to complete assignments by their due dates. Using long-term planners also increases your capacity to multi-task – you can be working on a current assignment as well as planning for the one due in four weeks' time.

Calendars

A cheap wall calendar can be an absolute saviour and, believe it or not, a potential peacemaker. It's visible, effective and won't 'die' and lose all your data if the battery runs out!

When I work with parents starting out on the secondary school journey, I always carry a little wall calendar with me – the one I use has a small whiteboard attached with a marker and is ready to hang up anywhere. I suggest that parents buy two – one for themselves and one for their son or daughter. When the work starts rolling in, suggest that your teen marks down what is due and when, and you make a copy of it. This is *not* invading their privacy. This is a work tool only, not a social calendar, and can be used in partnership with a planner.

Compare these scenarios:

1   Your son or daughter has a History assignment – you have a vague recollection of them complaining that this was a 'stupid' assignment and they didn't want to do it. You don't know when it's due, you have seen no signs of any research being done, no mention of progress, no requests for help...and you snap because you *know* there will be last-minute panic! "Don't you have a History assignment? Have you started it yet? I haven't seen you do any work lately and I would have thought you would be nearly finished by now. You haven't been anywhere near the computer, so I *know* you haven't been researching...what have you been doing?" Guess what the reaction will be? "Stay out of my life, Mum. I've got it all under control. You *don't know* what I've been doing. It's fine!"

2   Your son or daughter has a History assignment – you know it's due next week because you've seen it on your calendar. You're not sure how much work has been done – you haven't seen too much evidence of research and you would like to think a start has been made, but just in case..."I noticed you have a History assignments that's due next week. How's it all going? I'm assuming you've made a start. Do you need a hand with anything?" The reaction to this is likely to be far less confrontational and argumentative than that expressed in Scenario 1.

The assignment may still be sitting on the desk, untouched, and there may still be some last-minute panic to come, but the important thing is you have not assumed the worst and gone in on the attack. Because you have at least some idea about what's going on, you can open up a dialogue rather than start a war. When we speak about keeping open lines of communication with our teen, how much better is it to begin in a tone of concern and interest rather than a tone of accusation and angst?

What an amazing little peacemaker the humble wall calendar can be!

Diaries

Now, I like diaries – compact, heaps of storage and spaces where you can keep not only important dates, but also phone numbers, reminders, calendars and all sorts of cool information – even international dialling and time zones. Again, we have all sorts of electronic equivalents, but you can easily lose stored information in these...not in the old prehistoric hard copy versions! Call me old-fashioned...my boys do!

My biggest issue with diaries for students is that they don't use them properly. Many students, and parents, have admitted that they don't use them at all. A friend of mine once told me that she was so frustrated by her son's constant habit of handing work in late that she found his school diary and looked to see if he was noting down any dates at all. He was...but when he was *given* the assignment *not* when it was *due*. He was in Year 10.

Children in their final year at primary school are often given diaries, both to familiarise them with their use for secondary school, and to encourage them to start thinking more responsibly and independently as preparation for secondary school expectations. The main issue with most student diaries is that they are printed in a double-page spread, giving a one-week view. This is perfect for primary students as their work commitments rarely run for more than one week, apart from the occasional project. Secondary school is quite different, with almost all homework assigned as long-term tasks over several weeks.

To highlight the issue, I ask parents: "When your teen receives his or her first assignment, the date will be dutifully recorded in the diary. They are not familiar with looking beyond *one* week at a time. When do you think they will look at that due date again? The week it's due!" Hence, the need for a backup plan to remind them!

Most secondary schools insist on the use of dairies and these are often monitored by home room teachers, who sometimes write brief messages to parents or reminders to students in their diary. This is all well and good, but there is definitely a need for a more visual planning and reminder system as well.

'To-do' lists

The 'to-do' list is a little like a shopping list and can work very effectively for some students. Basically, you are simply writing a list of tasks which need to be done. It may be that subject tasks are mixed in together, ordered in priority. An example might be a student who has a History assignment due in Week 4 and a Geography assignment due in Week 6. The 'to-do' list for the week might list five items such as:

1   Edit draft History essay;
2   Draw History timeline;
3   Revise Maths for test Friday;
4   Check quotes for English essay;
5   Preliminary research for Part A of Geography assignment.

Once each task is done, it can be ticked off the list. Any item not ticked off goes straight to the top of next week's list – very easy!

Checklists

A checklist is a little like a 'chunking' planner. The student writes up a more detailed plan for the week in columns. The four columns might be headed:

1 Task (e.g. Geography research Part B);
2 Allocated time (e.g. 45 minutes);
3 Detail (e.g. geographical processes of a volcanic eruption);
4 Tick (done).

Each aspect of the task is designed to be done on one day, just not a specific day. It's a great feeling to tick off each task on completion and is also very motivating.

Research...it's an art!

Students entering the world of assignments, essays and research tasks are akin to the proverbial deer in headlights! Parents often feel the same.

For the most part, students in the primary or elementary years of education have limited experience of independent study or learning. Most homework tasks are short term and require minimal research. There may be set projects on particular social science topics, such as 'government', 'our community' or 'celebrations' and obviously these projects require research. Library sessions and computer lab time can often be utilised to conduct this research, with the end result being a beautifully written and decorated sheet of cardboard with all the required information crammed in between the diagrams, borders and fancy headings. The 'artistic' (some teachers would suggest 'cunning') students hide what might be an under-researched task in a wave of colour and grandeur.

It comes as quite a shock in secondary school when these students face the prospect of an assignment – with a word count! Parents are sometimes shocked as well, and many have reported to me a sense of resignation that they can no longer help. They can...but they should not *do* the assignment!

"It's like finding a needle in a haystack"

One of the biggest issues students have with the art of research is knowing *how* to find what they want. A parent recently approached me with what is a fairly common complaint: her Year 8 son had a Geography assignment to do and was beginning his initial research. He sat for two nights, about two hours each night, trying to find what he needed to make a start on answering the assignment questions. He was becoming increasingly frustrated, as was his mum, and finally walked away from the computer, lamenting "I can't find anything! I don't care about this stupid assignment anymore." Well, if that's not a research problem, a time-management issue and a potentially 'defeated' student, I don't know what is!

So, how do we help our kids discover the art of 'clever' research? Here are some tips to get them started:

1   *Brainstorm* what they know about the topic before they start researching – this requires them to write down what they already know about the topic – using single words, not sentences.
2   *Organise* these single words into '*themes*' or '*clusters*' relating to the assignment questions or topic they need to address.
3   Create a *chart, map or diagram* which has these word clusters organised around the central or key word or assignment topic.
4   Use some of these *key words* in your *search* for information.
5   To decide which site to investigate or which chapter to read, *skim* over the material to see if it's relevant – check *titles, sub-headings, diagrams, first sentence of paragraphs*.
6   If you decide that this particular resource is useful, *scan* the contents. Look for the specific information you need by *searching for key words* from the assignment; *ask* yourself some *questions* to determine relevance and then read a little more closely, but *don't read every word*.
7   Finally, *take some notes* rather than downloading or printing huge amounts of material. This will help you to *focus your attention*.
8   *Keep a record of your sources*.

It's amazing how a few basic steps can create a better attitude to an assignment which appears at first sight to be very involved, very long and, unfortunately for most students, very boring! We want our kids to work smarter rather than harder. Why labour away for additional hours? Effective research skills can take the load off them, the load off you, and free up time to do something a little more pleasant!

'Rocks, pebbles, sand' – a lesson to beat procrastination

This story is one that has been circulating the globe for years, and it's difficult to pinpoint its origin. It delivers a very powerful message about priorities and the important things in life...but it's also relevant to the life of a teen who always seems to be short of time.

There was a Philosophy professor who stood in front of his class one day and filled a jar with rocks. He told the class the rocks represented all the important things in life – family, friends, health, contentment, etc. – all the things we can't live without. He asked the class if the jar was full and they responded, "Yes".

He then took a handful of pebbles and asked if these could also fit into the jar, to which the class responded, "No." The professor placed the pebbles on the top of the rocks and shook the jar until the pebbles fell into the spaces left by the edges of the rocks. He told the class these pebbles represented the things we like, but could live without – wealth, cars, extravagant homes, expensive holidays, etc.

Finally, he took a handful of sand and said this represented the least important aspects of our lives, the things that sometimes get in the way of doing, or looking after, the important things. He sprinkled this sand over the top of the rocks and pebbles, shook the jar and the sand filtered through the small spaces in the jar.

The professor then told the class that if he had placed the sand in the bottom, then the pebbles and finally the rocks, he would not have had room for all the rocks. His message became clear. We must take care of the most important things in our lives first, then the things we would like to have or do and finally the 'small stuff' – if we have time.

We can apply this life lesson to the practice of prioritising rather than procrastinating. When an assignment comes home and it looks as though it will be a major time-consumer, it's a good idea to divide it into 'rocks', 'pebbles' and 'sand'.

The 'rocks' are the elements that will take the most time – the tasks which really are the foundation of the assignment, such as research. Identify these first and note them down.

The 'pebbles' are also critical to the assignment, and may include the drafting, editing, final writing or construction of the task. Identify these on a secondary list.

The 'sand' often includes the final elements, such as supporting sketches, quotes, labelled diagrams, etc....and bibliography. These are part of the assignment as well, but can wait till the end and won't require nearly as much time as the 'rocks' and 'pebbles'.

Once the elements of the assignment have been identified as 'rocks', 'pebbles' or 'sand', it becomes much easier to determine how much time to allocate to each. There is no point putting an enormous effort into the 'pebbles' or 'sand' if the foundational 'rocks' are not solid.

The bottom line is...school assignments and tasks are a fact of life. Procrastination is simply a recipe for anxiety and stress, but prioritising is a way of establishing control. A plan of attack is far more likely to lead to a feeling of success and well-being, but constant procrastination can only lead to an overwhelming feeling of anxiety and failure. Make a start on developing skills to combat procrastination before it becomes habitual.

Achievement is not only about high scores, it is also about progressing towards reaching the potential that is in every child, and the motivation to keep on keeping on. Parents can start the ball rolling by encouraging good work habits rather than nagging about the bad habits.

Maybe that Philosophy professor was fictional; maybe the story was true but time has erased his identity and details of the story. It's like a fable by Aesop – a great story with an important message, which we can apply to life and how we manage it.

In the words of Horace, the great Roman poet of the Augustan era, "He has half the deed done who has made a beginning". Horace was born in 65 BC and died in 8 BC...a pretty clever man, don't you think? If our kids won't listen to us, maybe they'll think it's cool to listen to someone who's been dead for more than 2,000 years!

LET'S SUM UP

The key to effective time management is having a *system* – one that works for you!

- Try a few different *time management tools* to get you started – planners diaries, checklists – use one or a combination.
- '*Chunk*' your work into smaller, more manageable tasks – it's important to feel you are making progress.
- *Procrastination* is the enemy! Once you *understand* the task, you've already started!
- Develop some clever *research skills* – reading techniques, brainstorming and mapping your ideas are all ways to get the job done and save time.

Chapter 9

Attitude – "What attitude?"

What is 'attitude'?

Attitude is all about how we perceive the world. When a young girl or boy is experiencing massive physical, emotional and cognitive change and also about to enter an entirely new system of learning, it's no wonder we, as parents, find ourselves at the receiving end of an 'attitude' we can often describe as unpredictable at best and hostile at worst.

I once heard famous American talk-show host, actress, media proprietor and philanthropist, Oprah Winfrey, say "The greatest discovery of all time is that a person can change his future by merely changing his attitude". There are times during our relationship with our young adolescents when we wonder exactly *when* there will be a change in their attitude; when we will see the re-emergence of our gorgeous boy or girl.

I am not a child psychologist or therapist. I can only relay some of the insights I have gained as a teacher and a parent, and pass these batons on to provide potential windows into your own pre-adolescent's behaviour and accompanying changes in attitude. If these messages and stories help you to reach your own personal epiphany, which then enables you to better understand the swings and roundabouts of your son's or daughter's attitude change, then I have done my job!

What do we know about 'attitude'?

Experience, education, personality, situations (and sometimes age) affect our attitude. What might annoy you as a parent might be perceived as acceptable, or even 'cool', by your pre-adolescent. Keeping in mind that your son or daughter is about to undergo a major change in learning, social circles and school environment at the same time as they are trying to test their independence from you, we should expect that the 'Clash of the Titans' may become a regular occurrence in your household.

Professionally, I can honestly say that the families who experience the least fall-out in this pre-adolescent period are the ones who have worked hard at developing a solid and positive relationship with their kids from the very beginning. Personally, as a parent, I can vouch for *honest communication* as being one of the most important building blocks in establishing a solid foundation for a relationship, which will no doubt have its share of tremors and quakes, no matter how strong you think you've made it. The important thing to remember is that once the quake has passed, your foundations are still standing with minimal damage.

My sons are no saints and there is no such thing as the perfect parent. I have dished out comments made in anger and I have had to cop the outbursts given 'with attitude' during these turbulent years. I haven't liked them and sometimes they hurt...and I have always told them as much. Sometimes the consequences applied for these outbursts were not popular, but when the young man finally emerges after the 360° head spins subside, you might be surprised by the comments they make, such as "What was I doing, Mum! If I was *my* kid, I probably wouldn't have been as patient as you!" Ahhhhh...gorgeous has returned!

Communication

There is no single, successful recipe for communication to suit every family and every individual within that family. I used to marvel at how two boys, born within 13 months of each other, with the same parents applying the same parenting techniques, could be so different! It's all in the genes. You could apply any number of theories to it – middle child syndrome, oldest child syndrome, youngest child syndrome, mixed gender siblings, single gender siblings, twins, home-birth babies, C-section babies, induced babies, older parents, younger parents, IVF parents...whatever theory you choose to apply to explain the differences in your kids, I don't care. They are what they are, and we have to cope with the differences!

While there seems to be no single, best way to communicate with your child, more specifically your pre-adolescent or adolescent, there are certainly ways to set the ball rolling if communication seems to have descended into the 'whatever' or eye-rolling stage. These are some of my tried and true (and more successful) strategies:

- Create opportunities to talk – *not* when either you or your teen is tired and/or angry.
- Some boys are more likely to engage in conversation if you are not looking at them! Unlike girls, who often respond to tone of voice, facial expressions and eye contact, in general boys don't much like the

eye-to-eye chat. You are likely to get a response when they're sitting in the back seat of the car or doing something with them (washing the car, playing a game…*not* shopping). Following an afternoon of monosyllabic grunts, a typical time for boys to pour their heart out is just as you are saying "Goodnight". Just as you are turning out the light or walking out the door (assuming that the room is already dark so you won't make eye contact) they will say, "Oh yeah, Mum, just wanted to tell you…". Now, you may have been heading out the door to reach for that long-awaited glass of wine or cup of tea – you've had a long day too and just want to switch off. My advice is – don't. Listen to your son; these opportunities won't come along too often if he thinks you have something better to do. Trust me when I say that the few minutes (or hours) sitting on the edge of his bed, in the dark, listening to what he wants to say will be repaid in spades in the years to follow. The cup of tea can wait.

- Some girls are more likely to internalise their worries than boys, so you need to keep an eye on any significant or ongoing changes in mood or behaviour. It is fairly common for girls to seek out the advice of their girlfriends. You don't have to suddenly become a 'girlfriend' if that is not the kind of relationship you have had with your daughter to date; but if you have some idea about what's worrying her, going in at an angle might help. So, rather than confronting her, approach the topic from a personal experience, a related incident…anything other than head-on.

- Your style of communication needs to be a little different now. Your views may not necessarily be theirs, so talk over your differences and try to reach some middle ground. If your son or daughter can see that you are prepared to listen and negotiate then you are more likely to earn their respect. Mutual respect is far more important than point-scoring and winning an argument over a difference in opinion. Whether you are right or wrong isn't really the issue; acknowledging that there is more than one viewpoint is the key.

- Avoid over-reacting. There will be times during this phase of development when your pre-adolescent will test your nerves and your patience, but be assured their defences will be up and ready to act if they feel you are constantly jumping down their throat. Of course you have your expectations and your rules, but remember this is not about winning all battles but about winning the war…and having both you and your teen on the same side at the end.

- Talk about what is important to them – I don't necessarily mean all the deep and meaningful issues, just simple, everyday stuff like their favourite music or bands; what new electronic games are popular; fashion trends; why current popular teen movies are popular, etc. You may be surprised by the respect you earn if you know the names of popular bands...and if you actually take the time to listen to some of their music, you are a star. I can remember Ben, in Year 8 at the time, coming home from school one day and saying how "cool" his friend thought I was because I had the car radio tuned in to a channel popular among teens, and I actually knew some of the songs. I didn't even know I was doing anything special, but I clearly earned some 'cred' that day!

- Be clear about your expectations for behaviour – have consequences; give reasonable choices; set limits – don't keep moving the goalposts just because it suits you at the time. If you want to establish or maintain a positive rapport with your young adolescent then you have a responsibility to communicate clearly, and negotiate if and when needed.

- Share some of yourself – not in the "back in my day..." kind of way, but personal anecdotes (even embarrassing ones) shared at the right time, in the right way.

- Don't nag. If you want to be respected as a team player and not an opponent, you need to earn it. I will give you an example:

TRUE TALES

This story relates to my son at 17 and in his senior school years, not Year 7. The message behind the story is, however, still relevant to the kind of communication we should be aiming for – right from the very beginning of secondary school.

Ben and I were discussing what we thought about the year ahead – what he wanted to achieve and how he was going to get there. I asked him what he wanted *me* to do for *him* to lighten the load. He answered very honestly and directly: "Mum, I want you to trust that I know what I'm doing. If I need help, or if you can see that I'm struggling, step in; if not, don't keep checking up on me. This last year of school will be all about how well I can cope with the pressure of what I'm expected to do, and it's starting already. Teachers put pressure on us to hand things in on time, do the best we can and keep the average up so we don't let the year cohort down; we pressure each other by constantly comparing results; and I put enough pressure on myself as well. What I don't need is to come home to more pressure. I want home to be my safety valve where I can relax if I want to."

After being so honest with me, I felt Ben deserved the same. "OK, that sounds fine with me, Ben, and I'm glad you told me," I responded. "But let me just say that you need to remember that we need reassurance too. We're not expecting that you give us a daily report, but don't shut us out either. Make sure you ask for help *before* anything becomes an issue, and let us know from time to time that you're OK." He agreed that we would soon know if there was a problem and that it was nice to know that we were now all on the same page – it made such a difference to that final, and quite stressful, year at school. It wasn't a perfect year by any means, but we knew we had each other's backs...we were a team.

Talk...and *listen!*

So far we have discussed a variety of forms of communication, but almost all of them have involved *talking*. Communication, especially with your pre-adolescent, is all about listening too. Transition to secondary school can be a pretty tough gig for some, and generally our kids are on 'information overload' by the time the new school year starts. We don't want to add our 'five cents' worth' when we should be listening instead of talking.

Active listening is a real skill – and sometimes it's hard for parents to STOP TALKING! We are often so determined to drive our point home that our kids switch off. Sometimes we just need to take a chill pill and listen.

The critical aspect of active listening[1] is allowing your son or daughter to hold the floor – without interruption. We need to just let them talk – even if it means taking mental notes of points you would like to add or questions you would like to ask – don't interrupt. By allowing your teen to completely unload – whether it's a rant about something that has happened at school; a tirade against something you've said or done; or simply telling a story – by allowing them to tell it all, uninterrupted, you have given yourself the golden opportunity to listen to it all, assess the whole picture and then possibly explore the problem (or find the solution) together. More importantly, they have opened up about how they feel – often a rare treat when you're living with adolescents.

So, this is how it works. After you have heard the whole story, you can clarify what has been said with a comment like, "From what you've said, am I right in thinking...?" This shows that you have indeed been listening and you understand the whole story. Then you might follow with a question such as, "It seems like you might be feeling a little...". This clarifies your understanding and may also acknowledge that there is some emotion attached to the story . Finally, you can ask a question like, "Have you thought about how you might handle...?" or "It seems you're unhappy with this situation. Am I right?" Communications expert, Sandra Boston, claims that a minor disagreement can erupt into a full-blown argument, "depending on whether we listen and respond, or react and control. A little skill and training make all the difference."[2]

An '*I-message*'[3] is another great form of communication. It is used to assert feelings or beliefs, but does not put the other person on the defensive or pass judgement. Dr Thomas Gordon, widely recognised as a pioneer in teaching communication and conflict resolution skills to parents, teachers and business leaders, developed what became known as the 'Gordon Model'[4] of parenting. Basically, this model of conflict resolution is based on effective communication techniques, rather than coercion. The technique of the I-message is fundamental to his model, as is active listening. Where active listening is effective when the *child* has a problem, the I-message is a technique *parents* use when *they* have a problem with the behaviour or attitude of their child.

This technique works quite well with teens who are often ready to challenge anything you say or do! Here are two scenarios – the first demonstrating the fairly common interaction between parent and, let's say, son. Scenario 2 uses the I-message technique.

1 James (let's say he is 12) has come home after spending the afternoon at a friend's house...or so you thought. He comes home two hours late and has obviously been to the beach. "I thought you were at Danny's place. I expected you home two hours ago," Mum snaps.

    "Well, we went to the beach. It was so hot today," replies James, still a little sheepish at this point.

    "Well, when I say home at six, I mean home at six. You had no right to take yourselves down to the beach without asking me first. You won't be going back to Danny's for a while because I can't trust you," Mum snaps again.

    "Yeah, typical. Do one thing wrong and it's all over. Don't you at least want to hear what happened?" James fires back.

    "No – I told you what I expected and you didn't take any notice," replies Mum.

    "Whatever – you don't care about anything I have to say anyway," grumbles James, as he storms off to his room.

2 James (let's say he is 12) has come home after spending the afternoon at a friend's house...or so you thought. He comes home two hours late

and has obviously been to the beach. "You're home. Looks like you've been to the beach. I thought you were going to Danny's house," Mum queries.

"Well, we went to the beach. It was so hot today," replies James, still a little sheepish at this point.

"Well, I did say to be home by six. I worry something's happened when you're late. If you had checked about going to the beach, I wouldn't have been so concerned about how late you are," says Mum, a little disappointed but calm.

"Yeah, probably should have thought to ring," replies James, "but Danny's mum had to take Jess there for surfing lessons so she offered to take us along," he added.

"Fine, but next time, please let me know just so I know you're OK," says Mum.

"Yep, sorry, Mum. Next time I'll tell you," finishes James.

I don't know about you, but Scenario 2 looks good to me. None of us can guarantee that it will play out this way every time, and the way we react often depends on our frame of mind and level of patience at the time. However, if we take a couple of minutes to think before we speak, we have a much better chance of keeping the door of communication open...rather than having it slam shut in our faces. The *thinking before we speak* rule is probably a good one to practise on partners as well!

Building a solid foundation for great communication with our kids shouldn't just start as they are approaching their teens. The earlier we start building a team approach with our kids, the better chance we have of keeping in touch when, developmentally, they start to look to their friends for advice rather than us.

Promoting a positive attitude to transition

Communication is a key factor not only in developing positive relationships in general, but also in preparing ourselves and our sons and daughters for the transition from one phase of education to the next...and nurturing an ongoing positive attitude to school in general.

In my experience, our kids generally feel more excited, more motivated and more ready for the transition to secondary school than parents. Often, *we* are the ones with questions, anxieties, doubts and sometimes 'baggage'. More often than not, parents say they have vague, but in general positive, memories of their early days at school but, for many, secondary school memories are not nearly as fond. Leave these memories aside when discussing the new stage ahead with your young adolescent.

This move to secondary school is a massive change, among all the other personal changes and challenges our young ones are already experiencing. The impact of school experiences on lifelong attitudes cannot be underestimated and it is important that, as parents, we remain switched on to ways we can support them.

Building on the positives

It is easy to be positive when you're around positive people – it rubs off on you. As parents we want to find every opportunity we can to build on our kids' strengths and work on the weaknesses. A few tips which might help *us* build on the positives include:

- *Valuing education* – despite our own past learning experiences, we need to constantly reinforce the importance of education and learning as a stepping stone to a future built on *choice*. If we have a negative attitude about school or what is being taught at school, our kids are likely to pick up on that – and we don't want to limit their chances of success because *we* have a bad attitude!
- During this middle years stage of development, our young adolescents are seeking both *challenge and relevance* in their learning. In simple terms, they are looking for their skills to be tested; they are looking for more independent learning; they are looking for a *reason* to learn what they're learning! This can be tricky for parents who are either unfamiliar with the different subjects studied in secondary school or who didn't like that subject at school either! A typical question will be: "Why do I have to do this stupid assignment? When will I ever need to know anything about wetlands?" Instead of making the fairly typical adult response of "I don't know; seems pointless to me" or "Yeah, I hated Geography too!" – we should be pointing out the *relevance* of the task, regardless of the content or topic. This is a great opportunity to remind our teen that at some point in the future they will have a boss who will ask them to complete a task – it may not be the task they would choose to do but they have a deadline. To complete the task on time they need to set up a plan and prioritise mini-tasks which lead to completion. *That's* what an assignment is teaching them, apart from increasing their knowledge of wetlands. If they don't get the job done – to the boss' satisfaction and on time – he or she might find someone else to do it!
- *Separate the adolescent from the school performance* – in a nutshell, as parents we need to acknowledge performance in a positive light rather than in a negative light. Remember that your young ones are stepping

into entirely new subjects, teaching methods and teachers. Research suggests that student academic decline is a common feature of this transitional period.[5] Instead of focusing on a mark or grade *not* achieved, focus on what *has* been achieved – an improvement, evidence of commitment to getting the job done, a study plan, effort. Acknowledgement that your young adolescent is achieving at some level creates the foundation for a positive attitude to learning and a commitment to continue the effort. If you complain about marks or grades not being high enough and take a "You can do better" approach you may end up with a student who fears failure, sabotages his or her own attempts at success or, even worse, completely disconnects from school and learning. We don't want to sugar-coat everything either – kids have a knack of seeing through fake messages. If effort is evident and results don't reflect that effort, we need to sit down with our kids and talk about how we can improve – goals are part of that plan, and are very successful in creating a positive approach to school in general, and learning in particular. If they need to step up to the plate and apply more effort, we can talk about that too.

Stop rescuing them! School, like any other environment, has its share of ups and downs along with its share of personality conflicts. We cannot fight every battle for them, just because they are moving into a world where they are now the 'little fish' in a much bigger pond. We need to remind ourselves that, just as we can't keep taking their forgotten lunches to school for them, we can't solve every problem for them either. I'm not suggesting that we throw them in the deep end, but steering them towards becoming resilient and independent young people, who accept that failure or challenge is part of living in the real world outside school, is enormously empowering. What we don't want to do is build a negativity into their thinking: "I won't volunteer to be part of the Year 7 band because I'm probably not the best drummer." Much better to think: "I'll have a go at being in the band. If they choose someone who's a better drummer than me, I might get a shot next time."

TRUE TALES

This highlights how close I came to 'rescuing' Adam on Day 2 of Year 7. I well and truly loosened the apron strings after this!

Day 1 of secondary school was hot, busy, confusing and very emotional...and that was just me! After seeing Adam wander off to his new Year 7 home room with his new Year 7 classmates, I felt quite disoriented and more than a little unsure of exactly what I was supposed to do from here on in. This was my baby…in secondary school!

Day 2 was pouring rain, cold, just as busy and confusing…and I couldn't find anywhere to park the car to drop Adam off as close as possible to the front gate. As he leapt out of the car and headed towards the gate, I noticed he had left his umbrella on the front seat. Too late to signal him, I decided to find a car space somewhere, and deliver the umbrella to him before the bell rang…after all, I needed to protect him from getting wet on the way home from school didn't I?

I parked the car, grabbed the umbrella and headed towards the gate. The first thing I noticed was how big some of these older students were! After so many years teaching children smaller than me, I very quickly understood how these new Year 7 students must be feeling when confronted with the fact that their new colleagues in education were young men and women…not really kids any more.

So, I walked around to the Year 7 area where they had all assembled yesterday and peeked around the corner of the brick wall to see if I could spot Adam. He was now attending an 'out of area' secondary school, with many of his friends attending a different school. There he was, standing on the outside of a circle of boys, trying his best to be part of the group, waiting for someone to acknowledge his presence and invite him into the circle.

I stood there for a moment or two – looked at him, looked at the umbrella, pictured a very wet and miserable 12-year-old coming home this afternoon and considered my options. To rescue or not to rescue. I'm glad to say I erred on the side of caution and took my chances with the rain – better to do that than face the aftermath of a poor decision!

When Adam arrived home that afternoon – cold, wet and miserable as predicted – I told him the story. "Mum, you didn't!" he gasped. "Stop rescuing," I thought to myself.

LET'S SUM UP

- Our *attitude* affects the way we *think, behave, view the world, think about ourselves* and *learn*.
- *Parents' positive attitude* can really make a *big difference* to the way our kids respond to the changes.

- *Communication* – fundamental to developing a *positive team approach*.
- *Talk and listen* – make sure you're getting *the right message* through *active listening*.
- *I-messages* clarify what we expect from our kids...in a positive way.
- *Build on the positives* about change – value learning and school; support resilience; separate the adolescent from the performance or result.

Chapter 10

Parents with style – which style suits you?

Is there such a thing as a 'parenting style'?

We all navigate our way through the parenting game differently. No one provided us with a manual for how to be the best parent, and we all do the best we can...and hope we get it right.

You probably haven't given much thought to labelling *how* you parent, but we generally fit into an identifiable style. As our children approach adolescence, it's a good time to reflect on *how* we are parenting, and if we need to grow and change a little along with our kids.

During the 1960s, US clinical and developmental psychologist Diana Baumrind conducted research on more than 100 pre-school age children. Observations, parent interviews and other research methods were used to identify particular methods or styles of parenting. She observed four key dimensions of:

1 disciplinary strategies
2 warmth and nurturance
3 communication styles
4 expectations of maturity and control

to determine three distinct parenting styles. These styles were identified as *authoritarian*, *authoritative* and *permissive*.[1]

In 1983, psychologists Maccoby and Martin[2] updated Baumrind's styles to include another dimension to parenting. They believed that 'permissive' parenting inferred 'indulgent' parenting, but there could also be 'negligent' or 'uninvolved' parenting associated with the broader term of 'permissive'.

Our own personal style of parenting can be determined by our upbringing, culture, educational level, personality, socio-economic status, family size, religion, etc. Of course, there may be diverse styles within the one family, with each parent perhaps favouring a different approach. If this is the case, it is really important for both parents to have a united front when determining boundaries, acceptable behaviour, expectations, etc. – and it doesn't get any easier when we are living with teens!

Where do you fit?

Authoritarian

The *authoritarian* parent is a parent in control…but not always with the best results. This is a parent who imposes absolute standards and expectations, with very little discussion on alternatives, and enforces punitive measures to curb behaviour. Parenting teens using an authoritarian approach is a little like waving a red rag at a bull – the rag-waver isn't happy and neither is the bull!

When our children are young, the authoritarian approach may get the response the parent seeks, with an obedient and submissive – but not necessarily a happy – child. The effect of this long-term authoritarian approach on kids is to create a foundation for low self-esteem, low social competence and a tendency to be more rebellious during adolescence. In fact, Diana Baumrind claims that "girls are particularly likely to give up and boys become especially hostile"[3] due to their poor reactions to frustration, and both boys and girls are more likely to be "anxious, withdrawn and have an unhappy disposition".[4]

If you are still not sure whether or not you fit into this category, think about how you respond to your son or daughter when you have reached an impasse – he or she wants one thing, you want another. Let's use the simple, and very common, example of cleaning their room.

Authoritarian scenario

You walk past your son's room and it is a mess. You have a rule that your kids' rooms are cleaned every Saturday morning. You bark at your son, "I want your room cleaned now!"

Son's response, "I know it's Saturday, Mum, but I don't have time now. I have an early soccer game today – I have to go."

"I don't care. The rule is that you clean your room on a Saturday morning…and it's Saturday morning. Do it now."

"Why *right now*?" queries son.

"Because I said so. My house, my rules. You'll still be in time for your game."

Now, there have no doubt been times when you have heard yourself say, "My house, my rules" or "because I'm the mum and I said so" – we all have days when our frustration overrules our tongues, and sometimes we find we have slipped into the role of Major Neat at all costs. However, if this scenario is typical of the way you negotiate with your adolescent, I bet there are constant fireworks at your house!

Authoritative

The *authoritative* parent has rules and boundaries – but can negotiate and is far more democratic, yet still assertive. There is a level of give and take in the authoritative relationship, where the parent shares the reasoning behind rules and boundaries rather than taking the "because I said so" approach.

Parents who assume an authoritative approach, especially when dealing with adolescents, are not necessarily immune from confrontation, but are more likely to reach a mutual agreement on at least *something*…rather than a "Mexican stand-off'. These parents have the happy knack of giving their child enough freedom of expression so that they can develop a sense of independence – they don't shut their kids down, but they don't let them rule the roost either.

One major difference between the authoritarian parent and the authoritative parent is the capacity and willingness of the authoritative parent to listen. When a young child breaks a rule, an authoritative parent is more likely to ask them why and listen to their response. An example might be, "You know you aren't allowed to go to a friend's house after school without telling me. Why did you do that?" Listening to the reasoning behind the poor decision is far more likely to lead to a positive reinforcement of the rules and a clearer understanding of why the rule is in place.

Similarly with adolescents (who are more likely to make silly decisions and poor choices because they just aren't thinking straight), we need to have consistency in our boundaries and a reality check on them from time to time. Have rules, but not unnecessary ones. Make the rules and boundaries important, with consequences in place for breaking the rules – but accept that your teen will slip up from time to time. If you have built a solid relationship based on unconditional love and fair, consistent boundaries you might still lose some battles, but you are more likely to win the war.

Research suggests that authoritative parents "monitor and impart clear standards for their children's conduct. They are supportive but not intrusive and restrictive. They want their children to be assertive as well as socially responsible; and self-regulated as well as co-operative."[5] If we use the same bedroom-cleaning scenario that we used for the authoritarian parent, it might play out something like this in an authoritative setting.

Authoritative scenario

You walk past your son's room and it is a mess. You have a rule that your kids' rooms are cleaned every Saturday morning. You call to your son, "You haven't cleaned your room yet."

Son's response, "I know it's Saturday, Mum, but I don't have time now. I have an early soccer game today – I have to go."

"Well, I don't want you to be late for your game, but couldn't you have organised yourself a little better to have it done before you go?"

"Yep, probably should have, but it's too late now," replies son.

"OK, but as long as you do it when you get home – it really is a mess in there and I want to vacuum today."

"I'll do it this afternoon – promise," son pledges as he darts out the door.

Permissive

The *permissive* parent, or 'indulgent' parent, makes very few demands on their children. More often than not it appears that the kids are in charge. This style of parent has few rules and rarely disciplines their child, often taking on the role of friend rather than parent.

Parents adopting a permissive style encourage their kids to think for themselves, avoid inhibitions and make decisions which are often outside their realm of maturity. While they are warm and caring parents, they are more switched on to their child's emotional and developmental needs than the need to set limits.

While permissive parenting might work on the home front, in the long term it doesn't help the child in the real world outside the home. These kids often have problems with authority and following rules and can underperform at school because they lack the persistence of others who have been more exposed to conformity and boundaries. They can be "rebellious and defiant when their desires are challenged",[6] are often reluctant to accept responsibility and have difficulty controlling their impulses.

Now, there will be times when we *all* become a little indulgent, especially with our young teens. They want something – we say 'no'; they come at us from a different angle – we still say 'no'; they come at us again and tug at a vulnerable moment (or when we have had a bad day) and we say 'OK, do what you want' – this doesn't make us a bad parent – just normal!

Let's look at the bedroom-cleaning scenario from a permissive parenting angle this time.

Permissive scenario

You walk past your son's room and it is a mess. You like the kids' rooms to be cleaned every Saturday morning. You say to your son, "You know I like the rooms cleaned on Saturdays. I need you to tidy up today."

Son's response, "I know it's Saturday, Mum, but I don't have time now. I have an early soccer game today – I have to go."

"OK – that's fine. I'll do it for you this week."

"Great – thanks. Could you clean my desk as well – I won't feel like it when I get home," replies son.

"No problem – enjoy your game," responds Mum.

Uninvolved or negligent

An *uninvolved* parent is one who makes few demands, communicates at a minimal level and is often detached from the needs of their children. They provide the bare essentials and often have little time or energy for their kids.

This style is the most destructive in terms of positive outcomes for kids. With so little commitment to effective parenting, "uninvolved parenting styles rank lowest across all life domains. These children tend to lack self-control, have low self-esteem and are less competent than their peers".[7]

If we place this in the context of teens and their sometimes irrational behaviour and thought processes, we can only fear for these kids.

TRUE TALES

In all my years of teaching I have just about seen it all – stories of triumph, disappointment, resilience, defeat, family conflict, family sadness and joy. One story sits high in my list of triumphs...a student who seemed destined to spend his life fighting his friends, teachers, parents and the 'system'. This was a student who had not been diagnosed with any psychological or emotional disorder, yet he was one of the most aggressive students I had ever taught. His mother had a kind heart and once said to me "I've done everything for him – I don't know why he is this way." Maybe *this* was the clue.

I first encountered, let's call him Nick, in Year 3 at a local state school where I was employed as a substitute teacher – I was not assigned any fixed class, but would rotate from class to class when teachers were absent or on leave. I had not taught Nick, but had certainly heard all about him. He was constantly being removed from the playground and was barely manageable in the classroom. He punched, he kicked, he swore at children and teachers alike – he was eight years old!

I had seen teachers physically struggling to remove him from the playground and he seemed to love the attention.

My first encounter with him in Year 4 was not pretty. He was defiant, unco-operative and a real handful – I couldn't wait for the day to be over. I used my teacher voice to try to assert some authority – didn't work. As I was not the regular classroom teacher, it was difficult for me to install any kind of real, meaningful, long-term consequences for behaviour, so I just had to tough it out.

When Nick was in Year 5, I was asked to relieve his classroom teacher for four weeks while she took some (no doubt well-earned) long-service leave. I fretted about my survival with this boy, and was offered much sympathy by the rest of the staff. Here was a boy who held both other students and teachers to ransom, and I was not about to become another 'victim'.

On the first day – Monday – Nick's table had been strategically placed right under the nose of the teacher, keeping him well out of the range of other students and neatly 'under wraps'.

Now, this was a boy who had never been given any responsibility or leadership roles at school – why would he, you ask? I knew I had to get him onside from the first day, otherwise it would be a very long four weeks. After the morning pleasantries, I marked the roll, with Nick staring at me with hooded eyes…no doubt wondering what he could do to disrupt the proceedings.

"Nick," I said, without looking up, "could you please take the roll to the office?" I could hear a couple of gasps, as Nick had done a 'runner' on more than one occasion. He looked at me in complete astonishment. "Do I take someone with me?" he asked. "No. You're a Year 5 boy, I'm sure you know where the office is and can get yourself there and back in a minute," I quipped. I knew this was a huge risk as Nick could have taken himself anywhere.

I must admit to having my heart in my mouth for the next 60 seconds…and then there was Nick, strolling back through the door and plopping himself dramatically back on his seat. "Thanks, Nick, good job. I'm sure there is probably a student who usually does that job, but give me time…it's my first day," I explained, "and anyway, doesn't hurt to change things around a little," I added.

That was the first act of responsible behaviour from Nick any of us had seen for a long time, and I continued to use him as a 'runner'. He was still aggressive towards other students and teachers in the playground, and I would often wander over and have a quiet chat with him when the dust had settled. It was always someone else's fault, according to Nick, and he couldn't admit that he had a problem with controlling his emotions. I wondered if I was getting through at all, but his classroom behaviour improved dramatically the more responsibilities he was given.

Nick was a tough kid, a little feared by other students, but on the final Monday of my four-week teaching block I walked into the room to find a picture of green hills, birds and a huge sun on my desk – all it said was "To Mrs Wilcock". I had no idea who it was from, so I watched the faces of every student as they entered the room to see if I could pick up a clue. As Nick sat down, he looked at the picture and then looked at me. I didn't say a word, knowing that he would be devastated if I thanked him publicly – he would never want his reputation to be softened. When the class started their work, I looked at Nick and gave a very subtle thumbs up, at which he smiled and looked away. I took him aside at recess and thanked him properly, telling him it would adorn my fridge when I got home.

My relationship with Nick proved one thing – given a chance, kids can do anything. His mum spoke to me soon after my four weeks and said how much Nick had enjoyed having me as his teacher. "You are the first one in a long time to trust him enough to give him a go. Maybe I should give him more responsibility at home and stop doing for him all the time." Her 'permissive' parenting, with all the good intentions in the world, had set Nick up to be rebellious and impulsive, always wanting his own way and defying authority in his attempts to get it.

It was amazing to see how a little accountability and responsibility, along with recognition for a job well done, had gone such a long way.

LET'S SUM UP

- Our *parenting style* is determined by a number of factors, including personal background and experience, culture, religion, socio-economic status, education and personality.

- There are three parenting styles – *authoritarian*, *authoritative* and *permissive*; *uninvolved* or *negligent* parenting has been identified as a sub-style of permissive.
- Children of *authoritarian* parents tend to be anxious, withdrawn, unhappy and don't respond well to frustrations. They generally perform well at school, but fear of failure can be the motivating factor for success.
- Children of *authoritative* parents tend to be confident, socially competent, independent thinkers with appropriate emotional regulation and a sense of responsibility and accountability.
- Children of *permissive* parents tend to be rebellious and defiant when needs are not met, have difficulty regulating their emotions, have low persistence and can display anti-social behaviours.
- Children of *uninvolved* parents generally underperform in many areas – academically, socially and emotionally; the result of a lack of boundaries at home and emotional detachment from parents often displays itself in poor behaviour and limited ability to form emotional attachments.
- We may need to *reflect on our style* of parenting, particularly as our kids enter adolescence, with a move towards the *authoritative* approach being far more effective.

Chapter 11

See it...hear it...do it – working smarter, not harder

Understanding how you learn

We might not *think* about how we learn – we just learn! During the early years of learning at school, memorising great amounts of content isn't so important. Most of the learning takes place in the classroom and is reinforced at home through a variety of homework tasks and projects. Our kids are constantly building their skills in literacy, numeracy, the arts, technology and science, physical education and the social sciences. What happens when they enter secondary school?

Welcome to a whole new world of study..."How do I study?" is a typical question posed by new secondary schoolers. It may not be the case worldwide, but at the elementary or primary level of education in Australia, students do not need to study for any exams as we don't have them. We have national assessments and internal school assessments, but no assessed tests which rely heavily on students memorising large amounts of content. So it comes as a massive shock when that first topic test or exam comes around in secondary school.

This issue of understanding learning styles is one I touch on in my workshops and it's always a winner. It's a topic we don't think too much about and it is always interesting to ask parents what advice they offer their secondary schoolers when they are quizzed about the best ways to study. The reaction is nearly always the same – "I just tell them what worked for me", is the typical response. But what worked for a parent might *not* work for their child, because we all learn differently.

What is 'learning style'

'Learning' is simply the art of acquiring and processing new information, and hopefully remembering it! There are various models and theories explaining how we learn and which method or 'style' is most effective for each individual learner.

Without drawing on too much detail, or favouring one theory over another, I think it is safe to say that some people learn best by seeing, some by hearing and others by doing. Sometimes there is a clear preference for one particular 'style', but not always. We are not necessarily locked in to one style for the rest of our lives – we can build on preferences, develop strengths in less preferred styles and sometimes we adapt to a less preferred style out of necessity. Certainly, in a classroom setting, it is quite easy to identify the different ways children use to learn and process information most effectively.

One of the best examples of seeing different learning styles in action was demonstrated by a class of particularly talented Year 5 and 6 children I had the pleasure of teaching several years ago. We were studying the Middle Ages and I gave them a long-term project to complete. I offered a variety of topics ranging from studying outstanding personalities of the day, such as Leonardo da Vinci, William Shakespeare or Joan of Arc; writing mock newspaper articles about the Crusades; designing a shield with a family crest; designing and building a Middle Ages weapon; giving a report on the causes and effects of the Black Death, and so on. They each selected a topic and were given eight weeks to complete the task. The results were outstanding!

Students chose topics that not only matched their interest, but also suited their style of learning. My 'little researcher' – a boy who was absolutely hooked on reading everything he could get his hands on covering almost every topic – researched Leonardo da Vinci in great depth. He presented a folder full of information and graphics and was happy to read some of the more fascinating discoveries to the class. Several boys took up the opportunity to design and build Middle Ages weaponry – from catapults to crossbows. One girl painted a wall frieze depicting a peasant family while another, our 'chatterbox', made a model of the Great Fire of London and stood in front of her classmates and described not only the model, but also the historic and tragic event in great detail – without referring to a single note.

These kids loved the experience and I'm sure still remember the details of their task because it meant something to them. Even more, they enjoyed the accolades from students from other classes who regularly took tours around our room, where every student's work was displayed. This was teaching and learning at its best! I am no learning style theorist, but I often wonder if those kids who constantly complain that school and, by association, learning are boring are given enough opportunities to learn in a way that suits them – that makes learning fun.

Visual learners

We would normally assume that visual learners are good readers. Certainly that is true of *visual linguistic* learners, who respond best to the written word. *Visual spatial* learners, on the other hand, respond better to graphs, charts and visual demonstrations.[1]

They also like to work in a quiet space and prefer to work alone, rather than in a group. Visual learners often like to keep lists as visual cues and frequently have good organisational skills. They are more likely to remember faces than remember the names of people to whom they have been introduced.

If you recognise that your son or daughter has a preference for learning and remembering material that is presented to them either in written or graphic form, it may be worth discussing a few techniques that might assist them in their study as they enter secondary school. Some of these tips might include:

- summarising notes in either written or chart form;
- highlighting key words in texts;
- visualising information;
- making flashcards with key words or abbreviated summaries for easier memorising;
- using symbols, cartoons or sketches to summarise material for easier memorising;
- visual cue-cards, such as sticky notes, placed around study areas to prompt memory.

Our younger son, Ben, has a very strong *visual spatial* preference. Rather than summarising texts in the form of bullet point summaries, he would colour code visual charts when revising large amounts of content. In preparation for his English exams at the end of Year 12, for example, Ben drew colour-coded charts of theme, character and context for Shakespeare's *King Lear* and was able to memorise the charts well enough to flesh out the detail to write an essay under exam conditions. Bullet point summaries were of little use to him.

Auditory learners

Is there such a beast as an adolescent who listens? At times we wonder! As with other learning styles there are also preferences *within* the style.

Auditory learning is, of course, the skill of learning through hearing the information. Unfortunately for those students who prefer to see or do, much of secondary school instruction is delivered verbally – great for auditory learners, but more difficult for others.

The most common auditory learner is the *auditory listener*. These are the ones who relate better to the spoken word; often they are impatient with written instructions or material and sometimes memorise best by rote.

The less common auditory learner is the *verbal processor*.[2] These are the learners who like to talk. They hear the information and will then happily repeat it, often in their own words, just to confirm that they have heard it correctly and understood it. Verbal processors love a debate, ask lots of questions in class (sometimes to clarify information, but not always) and like to voice their ideas while working through them.

Our older son, Adam, has a strong liking for verbal processing and was known to talk to himself from a very young age. I was quite concerned at first because he didn't appear to be talking to an imaginary friend; he was literally talking to himself...and answering! You know what they say about the first sign of madness.

After being convinced that there was indeed nothing wrong with Adam, I soon realised that this was his preferred way of processing and learning information. Whether it was something he had learned at school or following instructions on how to play a new game, Adam always preferred to repeat it – and if there was no one around to listen to him repeating it, he would repeat it to himself, generally aloud.

During his final preparation for Year 12 Biology exams, way out of my league of understanding, it was not uncommon for Adam to ask me to listen to all he knew about a particular topic. I can clearly remember one session during which he relayed all his knowledge of genetics – again, not a familiar topic to me, and cheerily announced on completion, "Gee, thanks Mum. That was a great help!" I had done nothing but stand there and listen, but for a verbal processor, this was study! This trend continues to this day and, when he is in the midst of developing some form of complex computer coding or simply trying to understand a new written task, he will openly talk his way through it. I just walk past his room and leave him to it.

A few tips which might promote more effective study for an auditory learner in secondary school include:

- reading notes and texts aloud;
- studying with a group; discussing the topic and asking each other questions;
- repeating information to be memorised to someone else;
- inventing rhymes or riddles to summarise information and then memorise;
- recording information to be memorised and listening to it repeatedly;
- re-writing summary notes and reading them as you write.

Kinaesthetic learners

We may think that all kinaesthetic, or hands-on, learners become our trades-people – builders, plumbers, electricians and so on, but this is not necessarily the case. Kinaesthetic learners also become our artists, dance teachers, aerobics instructors and so on.

Kinaesthetic learners absorb information best by doing.[3] They like to involve their body in the learning, either through movement or experience. In a classroom setting, it is difficult for these students to sit still for any extended period of time and they can appear to be distracted and fidgety. These learners need to keep busy. If you were to ask a kinaesthetic learner to complete a task that is unfamiliar to them, they are more likely to say 'I'll do it myself' than either read the instructions or listen to someone explaining how to do it.

Excursions and field trips are great learning tools for kinaesthetic learners. A trip to the zoo will be remembered in far greater detail than reading any amount of information on zoo animals or listening to a presentation on the topic. Kinaesthetic learners are also very expressive – they gesticulate, or use their hands, while speaking; they often speak quite quickly and they like to be on the move. I fear that, in the past, a number of students may well have been identified as suffering from an attention deficit disorder when in fact they were simply kinaesthetic learners. This is less likely to be the case now, as screening for attention deficit disorders is far more comprehensive.

Kinaesthetic learners like to chew gum or have something in their hands while studying or listening to aid concentration. It's quite typical for a hands-on leaner to be twirling a pencil or clicking a pen (annoying as that is) while they are listening to information or studying quietly on their own. Remove the gum, the pencil or the pen and the concentration is likely to be broken. As a teacher, I reflect on the number of times I have said to children, "I want everything out of your hands, eyes and ears to me and listen up!" I'm sure not all of the fidgets were kinaesthetic learners, but no doubt some of them were. I just hope I didn't impede their learning!

If you think you may have a kinaesthetic learner under your roof, and they are driving you mad with their restlessness and determination to be on the move all the time then these tips might help to establish an effective work pattern for them. Think about suggesting:

- dividing study or work times into shorter time frames – 20 minutes or so;
- planning to complete a certain amount of work within this time frame;
- taking a short break on completion of set work;
- using flash cards or cue cards to study – physically turn them over;

- recording material on a device and then going for a walk while listening/studying;
- typing summary notes on the computer;
- taking notes/highlighting in colour or drawing sketches of information – flow charts, etc.

TRUE TALES

This is a story which is probably not uncommon. This young man was in the final stages of his final year at school – and seemed to have no idea how to maximise his learning and study.

This boy could play the guitar brilliantly and had wanted to study music in his final two years at school. He was persuaded by family to study economics instead, because it was more likely to scale better when final results came through. Now, poor Jake hated economics and had been failing miserably throughout these last two years.

I was quite concerned about how he might be handling the study for this exam. He had failed his trial exam and things didn't look much better for the outcome of his finals. I asked if he would like a little direction in his study, to which he agreed.

Less than a week before his economics exam, I visited Jake to find him surrounded by economics books. He had the dining room table covered with textbooks, notes and study planners. There he was, sitting in the middle of it all, with pen in hand and open textbook in front of him. "What topic are you studying, Jake?" I asked. "Global economy," was his rather glum response.

I had never studied economics in my life – I came from an English/History/Languages background at school and right through university. My only economic achievement was the ability to balance a household budget!

"How are you going about studying for this, Jake?" I queried. "I'm just copying notes from the textbook in the hope that it sticks," replied Jake.

"Is it working? How many pages have you done?" I asked, while thumbing through his notes.

"I've written sixteen pages so far," smiled Jake, "but I don't know if I'll have time to even read through them again before the exam," he continued.

"OK, this isn't going to work. We need to look at some other way, Jake," I concluded.

I asked Jake how he usually studied for other exams and he admitted that at times it was hit and miss. He would usually just write summary notes and hope that he would remember enough to get through the exam with a pass. We then went on to look at a learning style profile to hopefully come to a better understanding of how Jake processed information. As it turned out, Jake had a preference for kinaesthetic learning, but also strong indicators of visual spatial. "I think we can kill two birds with one stone here, Jake," I commented, "and maybe even give you a better chance at a pass this time!"

I grabbed a piece of paper and asked Jake to tell me everything he could think of in relation to the topic of Global Economy – in no particular order and just single words. This was our brainstorm. He gave me around 30 words and I then asked him if these single words could fit into sub-topics or themes within this unit of Global Economy. Jake mentioned several sub-topics, such as Trade, Protection and Economic Development. "Would any of your words fit into these categories?" I asked. "Well, investment comes under Trade; tariffs and employment come under Protection; income, globalisation and sustainability come under Economic Development..." and so we went on.

We mapped out a chart of words and sub-topics under the main topic title of Global Economy and, by the time we had finished, Jake was very impressed with what he knew! In effect, Jake had scaffolded what he knew using minimal words – but was able to expand on these ideas verbally. This *visual spatial* activity suited Jake's style of learning and memorising and his *kinaesthetic* preference was also stimulated by active study. When I left Jake's house, he was a different, and much more confident, student.

Now, the fairytale ending would be that Jake, for the first time in two years, passed an economics exam. Unfortunately, the fairytale ending was not to be. Jake missed out very marginally on a pass – but he did score his best result in an economics exam for two years and his overall scaled exam score was boosted as a result. All this because he studied differently and understood a little better what made him tick as a learner. Working smarter, not harder, is the key!

LET'S SUM UP

- Learning is the skill of acquiring and embedding new material – and we all do it differently.
- We generally learn though seeing, hearing or doing – sometimes we have a *preference*; sometimes we use a *mix of styles*; sometimes we develop a

style because our work requires it. It's always good to *recognise strengths...* but also *strengthen your less preferred style.*

- *Visual linguistic* learners relate best to the written word; *visual spatial* learners relate better to charts, graphs, images, diagrams, etc.
- *Auditory listeners* relate well to the spoken word and can focus their hearing to learn new information; *verbal processors* like to repeat the information aloud or discuss.
- *Kinaesthetic learners* learn by doing; by being involved either physically, experientially or emotionally with the learning.

Chapter 12

The art of setting goals

Goals – are they important?

Whether we realise it or not, we set goals for ourselves several times every day. The simple task of catching that particular train, completing that task at work, making that long overdue phone call to a friend, explaining to your kids why you snapped back at them a little too quickly yesterday – all goals that we begin our day determined to achieve by the end of it. When you think about it, goals are central to our everyday lives. We need to remind our young adolescents of the value of goals as they enter this transition to secondary school phase, and it is certainly worth taking a few minutes to chat with them about what they would like to achieve in the coming year.

Without goals or targets, our kids can feel swallowed up by the changes they are experiencing in this new educational and personal phase. They need to feel that they can keep their heads above water – make new friends; keep up with the increased educational demands of secondary school; deal with the expectations of multiple teachers; not lose that map showing which building is where...and how to get there on time!

Goals are important to all of us and at critical times of change they are even more important. Goals are what motivate us, inspire us and point us in the direction we choose to follow. The earlier our kids value the importance of setting realistic goals for themselves, the more likely they are to maintain focus and the less likely to be overwhelmed by change and uncertainties.

Wishes and *goals* are not the same – we all *wish* for something, and it's often something we know is unlikely to be realised; but a *goal* is something different – with the right steps in place, the right motivation and the right amount of persistence and resilience, we *can* achieve – sometimes beyond our expectations!

SMART goals

The acronym *SMART* goals has been around for a long time. There are arguments as to where it originally surfaced and who 'invented' the acronym, but the term 'SMART goals' is definitely here to stay and is commonly used to frame the elements of goals quite simply.

When we think about setting goals for ourselves, we probably apply the SMART principle without even realising it. If we are discussing goal-setting with our kids, we probably need to identify the steps a little more clearly. As I often say to both parents and adolescents alike, it's easy to think about what we might *like* to achieve, but without some commitment to planning *how* we might achieve it, we are less likely to realise our goal. It's very easy to dismiss a thought, a goal, a desire without a plan – with a few steps in place, the goal suddenly becomes more achievable.

Specific

If we look at each of the elements of SMART goals, we can identify 'S' as being *Specific*. A specific goal is much more likely to be achieved than a more general goal. A workshop with a group of Year 9–12 students demonstrates this perfectly.

A Year 11 girl claimed she wanted to "get better marks in history". When I asked her how she planned to do that, she wasn't quite so sure. "You need to be more specific," I replied. "Is it the heavy content, the way you are studying, the amount of researching you are doing, the notes in class that need improvement?" She paused for a moment and then agreed that it was her lack of application in class. She simply wasn't taking enough notes. For the next few minutes she determined exactly *what* she needed to work on and how. Her goal had become more specific and less general, increasing her chances of improving in the particular areas of history she had identified.

When considering *specific* goals, we need to ask our kids to think about:

- what they want to accomplish;
- who else is involved in this specific goal;
- what are the benefits of achieving this goal;
- what are the obstacles to achieving this goal.

Measurable

The 'M' in SMART goals refers to the degree to which the goal is *Measurable*. If we can't see that we are making progress, and we haven't really thought about how we might assess our progress, it can seem like a very long road to achievement! If we work with our kids to initially establish and determine their goal and then apply some steps to measure progress, they will have a much better chance of sticking with it.

Achievable

Whoever we are, at whatever age, we want to set goals that have the potential to be realised. Our kids need to understand that there is little point in setting a goal which is outside their capacity to achieve – one that relies too heavily on others for support or one that is outside their control.

It is also critical to remember that for goals to be *achievable*, they also must be important to the person setting them. It doesn't matter what you, as a parent, teacher, coach or friend believe your son, daughter, student, player or friend is capable of achieving...if they don't want it, they won't achieve it. I have encountered many parents who have made comments to me such as "I think she would be great in the school debating team. I want her to volunteer, but she won't." She won't because it is not something that's important to her at this time. Later, perspectives might change but, if not, don't push it!

Realistic

To be a *realistic* goal, it must be one which your adolescent is willing and able to work towards achieving. Some goals take longer to achieve than others, so if the goal is unrealistic there is certainly an increased risk that it will fall by the wayside before it is achieved.

To decide whether a goal is realistic or not, it's probably a good idea to chat with your teen about what, if any, obstacles might either slow the progress of achievement or block it altogether. Once they have thought about this, they can then modify the steps they have planned to achieve the goal, or redefine exactly what it is they hope to achieve.

Time-framed

There is not much point in setting a goal that doesn't have a time limit. Without a time frame, there's no real sense of urgency. "Someday I'd like to…" is more like wishful thinking than goal-setting. Establishing a reasonable time frame helps them plan their progress and prioritise their steps towards achievement. They might have a time frame of weeks, months or years for a long-term goal, but obviously shorter time frames for short-term goals.

Short-term and long-term goals

The easiest way to describe the difference between short- and long-term goals is to use an example.

Let's say you have a budding athlete who, at 13 years of age, announces she would like to run at the Olympics, which are four years away. Clearly, her *long-term* goal is to compete in the Olympic Games.

Four years is a very long time to maintain focus on achievement, without some *short-term* goals or plans to make it happen. It would be pointless to say to this young athlete, "Well, I guess you will have to train really hard for the next four years and hope you can reach the qualifying time for selection." The prospect of running literally thousands of kilometres over the next four years is not very inspiring, nor very productive in terms of measuring progress.

So, what might her coach suggest as *short-term* goals? It may be that the coach feels that she needs to improve her endurance if she wants to focus on the middle-distance events. A *short-term* goal might be to focus on running for distance rather than for time, and over the next winter season she will run every second day and log her distance, not her time.

Once her endurance has developed, the coach might then focus on incorporating speed into her training programme and monitor her progress over short distances. She is very inexperienced at racing, so her coach sets a timetable of introductory and age-appropriate races – not Open National Championships in her first year of racing!

Over a period of four years, the short-term goals change as each goal is reached, and progress is made. She is ultimately working towards the *long-term* goal of running at the Olympic Games in four years' time.

Sometimes we aren't very patient – and teens are no different. Long-term goals are far more difficult to achieve without a plan, whereas short-term goals, by their very nature, are timetabled to be achieved within a shorter time frame.

If we encourage our kids to link short-term goals to their long-term goals, they are more likely to stay on track. It is such a good feeling to achieve short-term goals, and know that you are progressing towards the long-term goal you have set your mind on achieving. Even if the long-term goal changes or is abandoned or replaced along the way, the sense of satisfaction at achieving short-term goals is not to be underestimated.

However, *not all short-term goals are linked to a long-term goal*. Some short-term goals can stand alone. For example, your teen may have an assignment that is due in two weeks' time, but their goal is to complete it by the end of the first week. They carefully plan their time and the goal is achieved.

When working with students who are anxious about leaving old friends when moving on to secondary education, quite often I offer this as a simple short-term goal: say hello to at least one new student each day, and smile while you're saying it! The goals don't need to be huge, they just need to be important to the person who sets them.

Why are goals important?

Without goals, we have little direction – no purpose but just to plod through every day and hope it's a good one. Setting goals is a great motivator – it helps us to decide what is important to us and what's not; it helps us focus our energies on planning and achieving; it gives us confidence and self-satisfaction when we have achieved our goals.

Sadly, there are many kids who sabotage their chances of success by not committing to even considering setting a few goals. Sometimes this fear of commitment is based on a lack of self-confidence and sometimes it can be through fear of disappointing a parent, a teacher, someone who matters to them.

This transitional phase is all about uncertainty and change; but it is also about self-awareness, growth, development and chances for a fresh start and opportunities to shine. As a parent, we can take a role by opening up discussions around what your young teen wants from this secondary school experience. Avoid the high-energy 'you can take on the world' approach. In general, young teens just want to fit in, not stand out. They are feeling their way in a new educational environment among new peers and they want to slot nicely into their new surroundings. Making their way from being the big fish in a small pond to the tadpoles in a river is a major process…guide them towards thinking about what *they* want, not what you want for them. Success is far more likely if you do.

TRUE TALES

I asked a group of Year 6 students one day what they wanted to achieve in Year 7. Now, keeping in mind that they were the school leaders with no experience outside this little fish bowl, the responses were typically grand.

One of the students in this class was something of an 'Einstein'… and he knew it! His hand shot up immediately. "Yes, Dan, what's one of your goals for next year?" I asked.

"Well, I'm really good at maths and have topped the class all year. I want to be the best at maths in Year 7," replied Dan, brimming with confidence.

"Sounds like a big goal, Dan. Any idea how you might plan for it?" I quizzed.

"Not really, I don't think it will be too hard," he said smugly.

I didn't want to 'kill' Dan's enthusiasm for success, but I wanted to make him think about how he might go about achieving this goal... and also think about a few more simple, short-term and immediately achievable goals to help settle in comfortably to a new school at a more personal and less academic level.

"OK, Dan. You will need to start by looking at one maths topic at a time and work through each topic to the best of your ability. That might be one way to experience small successes along the way to hopefully achieving your long-term goal for this year," I suggested. "But, Dan," I continued, "you know how upset you are every time you forget your lunch and leave it at home. Why not make it a short-term goal to remember to pick your lunch up from the bench each morning? That way you won't feel upset and possibly embarrassed among your new classmates."

Dan flushed just a little and said, "Yeah, probably a good idea. I guess I can take the maths one topic at a time." Point taken!

Goals don't always need to be lofty and impressive – meaningful and achievable makes much more sense.

LET'S SUM UP

- When setting a goal you need to *define it*, *outline the steps* to achieve it, *monitor progress*, *set deadlines* and *review* your goal from time to time.
- Goals need to be *important to your teen* – not you!
- *SMART* goals give direction and purpose – *specific, measurable, achievable, realistic* and *time-framed*.
- *Long-term* goals are often our most meaningful goals – they require *planning* and *commitment*.
- *Short-term* goals can be *stand-alone* goals or *stepping stones* for long-term goal achievement.
- Goals *motivate* us to reach higher and give us enormous *confidence* and *satisfaction* once achieved.
- *Parents* can play a *role in guiding* their teens towards considering setting meaningful and achievable goals – *open up the conversation!*

Epilogue – the last word

Parenting, living and working with young people can be a tough gig at times – but it can also give you the most stimulating and enthralling ride of your life!

If you have picked up just one tip, strategy, idea, notion or inspiration from this book to ease the ride, then that's great. If what you have read has simply confirmed what you already knew...that you are on the right track...even better.

Celebrate the differences and uniqueness of your kids and never forget what an impact you have on them. Your experience, your words of wisdom, and your humour might not always seem to hit the mark – but it's amazing how your own words come back to you when you least expect them. They *do* listen!

Transition to secondary school is a new and exciting phase – embrace it with your kids and remember you are both on the same side.

Notes

Introduction

1 P. Hill and V. J. Russell, 'Systemic Whole-school Reform of the Middle Years of Learning', *Enhancing Educational Excellence, Equity and Efficiency: Evidence from Evaluations from Systems and Schools in Change*, Dordrecht: Kluwer Academic Publishers, 1999, pp. 167–196.
2 E. M. Anderman and M. L. Maehr, 'Motivation and Schooling in the Middle Grades', *Review of Educational Research*, Vol. 64, 1994, p. 287.
3 A. Martin, *How to Motivate your Child for School and Beyond*, Australia: Transworld Publishers (Division of Random House, Australia), 2006, p. 213.
4 Ibid., pp. 34–35.
5 S. Hollingworth, K. Kuyok, A. Mansaray and A. Rose, 'An Exploration of Parents' Engagement with their Children's Learning', *Institute for Policy Studies in Education*, London Metropolitan University, 2009, pp. 61–63. Available at http://dera.ioe.ac.uk/10475/1/parents_engagement_children_final.pdf [accessed 7 July 2012].
6 M. D. Levine, *Ready or Not, Here Life Comes*, New York: Simon & Schuster Inc, 2005, p. 201.
7 Ibid.

I The middle years – morphing from gorgeous to grumpy

1 M. Spellings, *Helping your Child through Early Adolescence*, Washington DC: US Department of Education, Office of Communications and Outreach, 2002, pp. 4–5.
2 R.E. Dahl, 'Adolescent Brain Development: A Period of Vulnerabilities and Opportunities', *Annual New York Academy of Science*, 1021, 2004, pp. 1–22.
3 J. Giedd, 'Inside the Teenage Brain', PBS Frontline interview, uploaded 15 November 2007. Available at http://www.pbs.org/wgbh/pages/frontline/shows/teenbrain/interviews/giedd.html [accessed 7 July 2012].

2 Girls and boys – *vive la différence*!

1 D. Chadwell, 'Engaging the Differences Between Boys and Girls', *Middle Matters*, March, Vol. 15, No. 4, 2007, pp. 1–3.

2 M. Gurian and K. Stevens, 'With Boys and Girls in Mind', *Educational Leadership: Closing Achievement Gaps*, November, Vol. 62 , No. 3, 2004, pp. 21–26.
3 W. McBride, *Boys will be Boys and Girls will be Girls: Teaching to Gender Differences*, Nashville, TN: Incentive Publications Inc, 2009, p. 2.
4 Ibid.
5 Al Roker interviews Leonard Sax on *Why Gender Matters*, uploaded 15 November 2007. Available at http://www.youtube.com/watch?v=eXqiJLZm-DI [accessed 7 July 2012].
6 McBride, op. cit., p. 4.
7 L. Sax, *Why Gender Matters – What Parents and Teachers Need to Know About the Emerging Science of Sex Differences*, New York: Broadway Books, 2005, p. 25.

3 The new social network – real friends, not online!

1 M. Evangelou, B. Taggart, K. Sylva, E. Melhuish, P. Sammons and I. Siraj-Blatchford, 'What makes a Successful Transition from Primary to Secondary School?', *Effective Pre-School, Primary and Secondary Education 3–14 Project (EPPSE 3–14)*, Department for Children, Schools and Families (UK), 2008, pp. 1–23.
2 Ibid., p. 16.
3 J. Lehman, 'Does your Child have "Toxic" Friends?'. Available at www.empoweringparents.com/Is-Your-Child-or-Teen-Hanging-Out-With-the-Wrong-Crowd.php [accessed 7 July 2012].

4 Parents keeping a connection with their school

1 W. H. Jeynes, 'Parental Involvement and Student Achievement: A Meta-analysis', *Family Involvement Research Digest*, Cambridge, MA: Harvard Family Research Project, 2005. Available at http://www.gse.harvard.edu/hfrp/publications_resources/publications_series/family_involvement_research_digests/parental_involvement_and_student_achievement_a_meta_analysis [accessed 7 July 2012].
2 S. Hollingworth, K. Kuyok, A. Mansaray and A. Rose, 'An Exploration of Parents' Engagement with their Children's Learning', *Institute for Policy Studies in Education*, London Metropolitan University, 2009, p. 19. Available at http://dera.ioe.ac.uk/10475/1/parents_engagement_children_final.pdf [accessed 7 July 2012].

5 Aligning the stars – finding that balance between work and play

1 K. Kruszelnicki, 'Teenage Sleep', 2007. Available at http://www.abc.net.au/science/articles/2007/05/03/1913123.htm [accessed 7 July 2012].

6 Work environment – basic or brilliant?

1 Heschong Mahone Group Inc, 'Daylighting in Schools. An investigation into the relationship between daylighting and human performance', Fair Oaks, CA, 1999, pp. 24–29. Available at http://www.h-m-g.com/downloads/Daylighting/schoolc.pdf [accessed 7 July 2012].

2 R. J. Paget, *The Role of Music in Learning*, Birmingham, UK: BAAT Ltd, 2006, pp. 5–6. e-Book available at http://www.baatltd.com/newsletters/The%20Role%20of%20Music%20in%20Learning.pdf [accessed 7 July 2012].

9 Attitude – "What attitude?"

1 T. Gordon, *Parent Effectiveness Training*, USA: Random House Paperbacks (30th edn, 2001), 1970, pp. 106–114.
2 S. Boston, *Aiming your Mind: Strategies and Skills for Conscious Communication*, Greenfield, MA: self-published, 2007, p. 5.
3 Gordon, op. cit., pp. 138–160.
4 Gordon Model of Parenting. Available at http://www.gordontraining.com/parent-programs [accessed 7 July 2012].
5 C. McGee, R. Ward, J. Gibbons and A. Harlow, *Transition to Secondary School: A Literature Review*, Hamilton, New Zealand: Waikato Institute for Research in Learning and Curriculum, School of Education, University of Waikato, 2003, p. 3. Available at http://www.educationcounts.govt.nz/publications/schooling/5431 [accessed 7 July 2012].

10 Parents with style – which style suits you?

1 D. Baumrind, 'Effects of Authoritative Parental Control on Child Behaviour', *Child Development*, Vol. 37, No. 4, 1966, pp. 887–907.
2 E. E. Maccoby and J. A. Martin, 'Socialization in the Context of the Family: Parent–Child Interaction', in P. H. Mussen and E. M. Hetherington, *Handbook of Child Psychology: Vol 4. Socialisation, Personality and Social Development*, 1983, 4th edn, New York: Wiley.
3 D. Baumrind, 'Child Care Practices Anteceding Three Patterns of Preschool Behaviour', *Genetic Psychology Monographs*, 75, Vol. 1, 1967, pp. 43–88.
4 Ibid.
5 D. Baumrind, 'The Influence of Parenting Style on Adolescent Competence and Substance Use', *Journal of Early Adolescence*, Vol. 11, No. 1, 1991, pp. 56–95.
6 D. Baumrind, 'Child Care Practices Anteceding Three Patterns of Preschool Behaviour', pp. 43–48.
7 E. E. Maccoby, 'The Role of Parents in the Socialisation of Children: An Historical Overview'. *Developmental Psychology*, Vol. 28, 1992, pp. 1006–1017.

11 See it…hear it…do it – working smarter, not harder

1 M. L. Conner, *Learn More Now*, New Jersey: John Wiley and Sons Inc, 2004, pp. 38–50.
2 Ibid.
3 Ibid.

Bibliography

Baumrind, D., 'Child Care Practices Anteceding Three Patterns of Preschool Behaviour', *Genetic Psychology Monographs*, 75(1), 1966.

Baumrind, D., 'Effects of Authoritative Parental Control on Child Behaviour', *Child Development*, 37(4), 1966.

Baumrind, D., 'The Influence of Parenting Style on Adolescent Competence and Substance Use', *Journal of Early Adolescence*, 11(1), 1991.

Boston, S., *Aiming Your Mind: Strategies and Skills for Conscious Communication*, Massachusetts: self-published, 2007.

Chadwell, D., 'Engaging the Differences Between Boys and Girls', *Middle Matters*, March, 2007, Vol. 15, No. 4.

Conner, M. L., *Learn More Now*, New Jersey: John Wiley and Sons, Inc, 2004.

Dahl, R. E. 'Adolescent Brain Development: A Period of Vulnerabilities and Opportunities', *Annual Academy of Science*, 1021, 2004.

Evangelou, M., Taggart, B., Sylva, K., Melhuish, E., Sammons, P. and Siraj-Blatchford, I., 'What Makes a Successful Transition from Primary to Secondary School?', *Effective Pre-school, Primary and Secondary Education 3–14 Project*, Department for Children, Schools and Families (UK), 2008.

Giedd, J., 'Inside the Teenage Brain', PBS Frontline online interview, 2002.

Gordon, D., *Parent Effectiveness Model*, USA: Random House Paperbacks, 1970 (30th edn, 2001).

Gurian, M. and Stevens, K., 'With Boys and Girls in Mind', *Educational Leadership: Closing Achievement Gaps*, November, 2004, Vol. 62, No. 3.

Heschong Mahone Group Inc., 'Daylighting in Schools. An Investigation into the Relationship between Daylight and Human Performance', Fair Oaks, California, 1999.

Hollingworth, S., Kuyok, K., Mansaray, A. and Rose, A., 'An Exploration of Parents' Engagement with their Children's Learning', *Institute for Policy Studies in Education*, London: London Metropolitan University, 2009.

Jeynes, W. H., 'Parental Involvement and Student Achievement: A Meta-analysis', *Family Involvement Research Digests*, Cambridge, MA: Harvard Family Research Project, 2005.

Kruszelnicki, K., 'Teenage Sleep', online ABC Science, 2007. Available at http://www.abc.net.au/science/articles/2007/05/03/1913123.htm [accessed 7 July 2012].

Lehman, J., 'Does your Child have "Toxic" Friends'. Available at http://www.empoweringparents.com/Is-Your-Child-or-Teen-Hanging-Out-With-the-Wrong-Crowd.php [accessed 7 July 2012].

McBride, W., *Boys will be Boys and Girls will be Girls: Teaching to Gender Differences*, Nashville, TN: Incentive Publications, Inc., 2009.

Maccoby, E. E., 'The Role of Parents in the Socialization of Children: An Historical Overview', *Developmental Psychology*, 28, 1992, pp. 1006–1017.

Maccoby, E. E. and Martin, J. A., 'Socialization in the Context of the Family: Parent–Child Interaction', in P. H. and E. M. Hetherington, *Handbook of Child Psychology: Vol. 4. Socialisation, Personality and Social Development* (4th edn), New York: Wiley, 1983.

McGee., R., Ward, R., Gibbons, J. and Harlow, A., 'Transition to Secondary School: A Literature Review', Hamilton, New Zealand: Waikato Institute for Research in Learning and Curriculum, School of Education, University of Waikato, 2003.

Paget, R. J., *The Role of Music in Learning*, Birmingham, UK: BAAT Ltd, e-book, 2006.

Spellings, M., *Helping your Child through Early Adolescence*, Washington DC: US Department of Education, Office of Communications and Outreach, 2002.

Index

attitude 73
    positive 79–80

brain 7–8
    amygdala 7
    corpus callosum 11
    'grey matter' 7
    left brain 12
    McBride, William 12
    melatonin 36
    myelination 7
    neuron 7
    right brain 11
    synapse 7
    synaptic pruning 7

communication 9, 36–8, 74–6
    active listening 77
    I-messages 78
    Lehman, James 22
    Total Transformation Program 22
community 27
    barriers 27–8
    'connect' 26–7
    engagement 27
    involvement vs engagement 25–6
    parent–school partnerships 24

development
    adolescence 4–6
    cognitive 6
    emotional 4
    Levine, Mel 2
    middle years 3
    physical 4
    puberty 4
    social 5

friendships 18
    making new 17
    peer groups 6
    'wrong crowd' 21

gender differences 12–14
    hormones 4
    Sax, Leonard 12
goals 42, 101
    achievable 103
    long-term 104–5
    measurable 102–3
    realistic 103
    short-term 104–5
    SMART 102
    specific 102
    time-framed 103

learners
    auditory 45, 96
    kinaesthetic 45, 97–8
    visual 45
    visual linguistic 95
    visual spatial 95
    verbal processor 96
learning 'style' 93–5
lifestyle
    balance 34
    circadian rhythm 36
    diet 35
    healthy 34–5
    routine 39
    sleep 35–6

motivation 1
    achievement 1–2
    Martin, Andrew 1

motor skills
  fine 13
  gross 13

organisation 53
  diaries 59, 66–7
  folders 59
  planners 59, 65
  storage 48, 60

parents
  authoritarian 86–7
  authoritative 87–8
  Baumrind, Diana 85
  involvement 27
  limits 8
  parent 'hub' 29
  parent 'style' 85
  permissive 88–9
  uninvolved 89

time management 61
  'brainstorm' 69
  calendars 65–6
  checklists 68
  'chunk' 62–3, 71
  lists 'to do' 67
  procrastination 62
  research 68
transition 1–2
  research 17

workspace
  distractions 49
  lighting 46
  music 49
  study space 48–9
  ventilation 47